THE PROBLEM OF SLAVERY
IN EARLY VERMONT,
1777–1810

The Constitution of Vermont

HARVEY AMANI WHITFIELD

THE PROBLEM OF SLAVERY IN EARLY VERMONT, 1777–1810

VERMONT HISTORICAL SOCIETY   Barre, Vermont

Cover image: Letter of Levi Allen to Jacob Lansingh (1784).
Frontispiece: The 1777 Vermont Constitution.

Copyright © 2014 by Harvey Amani Whitfield

Library of Congress Cataloging-in-Publication Data

The problem of slavery in early Vermont, 1777-1810 / Harvey Amani Whitfield.
    pages cm
  Includes bibliographical references and index.
  ISBN 978-0-934720-62-5 (alk. paper)
  1. Slavery--Vermont--Sources. 2. Slaves--Vermont--Sources. 3. Vermont--Race relations--History--18th century--Sources. 4. Vermont--Race relations--History--19th century--Sources. I. Whitfield, Harvey Amani, 1974- editor of compilation, author.
  E445.V4P76 2013
  306.3'620974309033--dc23

2013043156

Printed in the United States of America
27 26 25 5 6 7

Designed by Ann Aspell
Fifth Printing, October 2025

ISBN: 978-0-934720-62-5

CONTENTS

Carey's American Pocket Atlas (Philadelphia: Printed for Matthew Carey, by Land and Ustick, 1796). *Courtesy of Special Collections, Bailey/Howe Library, University of Vermont.*

Preface

This short monograph examines the persistence of slavery in Vermont after the 1777 constitutional abolition provision. The chaotic and gradual end of slavery is traced through an examination of Vermont census records, court documents, government legislation, bills of sale, runaway advertisements, and town records. In exploring the end of slavery, the book highlights the problematic establishment of freedom, which left many Afro-Vermonters in a difficult situation where they could find freedom and opportunity, but also slavery, reenslavement, and deeply rooted levels of racial discrimination.

The Problem of Slavery in Early Vermont, 1777-1810 is meant for an educated (not simply scholarly) audience with interest in the Green Mountain State's history. What emerges from this work is that black history and race relations in Vermont were complicated and contingent, especially as the state worked to abolish the vestiges of slavery in the late eighteenth and early nineteenth centuries. This assertion may not fit easily into the popular notion of Vermont as the first region in North America to completely abolish slavery and offer rough equality for African Americans. In fact, the state is home not only to a rich abolitionist history, but also to the more troublesome story of slavery.

NOTE ON TERMINOLOGY

The literature on the meaning of race and racism as well as the definition of slavery is vast.[1] One widely recognized authority, Orlando Patterson, defined slavery as "the permanent, violent domination of natally alienated and generally dishonored persons."[2] Patterson did not believe that slavery could be understood simply as a property relationship. But while Patterson's definition is useful, a precise meaning of "slavery" is problematic to pin down because the institution has been practiced in different ways and various contexts throughout human history. In the North American context during the late eighteenth century, slavery usually meant the control, chattel ownership, and appropriation of one person's labor by another person, which was given the force of law. Broadly speaking then, slavery can be framed and understood as the legal, violent, or permanent exploitation of another person's life, labor, and offspring. In Vermont, even after the 1777 constitution outlawed adult slavery, some black people were enslaved who legally should have been free. These people suffered from *de facto* slavery, a form of bondage not sanctioned by law that involved the forceful exploitation of an individual. In Vermont, masters exploited these *de facto* slaves by appropriating their labor, buying and selling them, and restricting their freedom of movement despite the fact that the Constitution of 1777 had granted them freedom. The experience of Judge Jacob's Dinah is an excellent local example of *de facto* slavery (see Document 27).[3]

"Racism" remains a hotly contested scholarly term. In his book, *The Forging of Races*, Colin Kidd emphasizes the dangers of trying to precisely define racism, noting that it is "unhelpful" to begin "with a set of rigidly defined concepts."[4] Although Kidd makes a valid point, one can generally say that racism relies on the application of a set of negative characteristics from one group to another based on skin color. Racism can be based in both ethnicity and biology—the assumption that one's behavior, intelligence, and ability are determined by her or his "race." In the context of this study, many Vermonters probably saw black people as different and possibly unequal, but this view had more to do with perceived racial or color difference than with any sort of biological view of the inherent and unchanging inferiority of black people. Indeed, scientific or biological racism became much more prevalent in the nineteenth century than it had been in the late eighteenth century.

1. The literature about race, racism, and slavery is vast and cannot be covered in detail here. It includes, but is not limited to the following: Mark M. Smith, *How Race is Made: Slavery, Segregation, and the Senses* (Chapel Hill: University of North Carolina Press, 2008); Ira Berlin, *Many Thousands Gone: The First Two Centuries of Slavery in North America* (Cambridge, Mass.: Harvard University Press, 1998); Joanne Pope Melish, *Disowning Slavery: "Race" and Gradual Emancipation in New England* (Ithaca, N.Y.: Cornell University Press, 1998); Colin Kidd, *The Forging of Races: Race and Scripture in the Protestant Atlantic World, 1600-2000* (Cambridge: Cambridge University Press, 2006); David Armitage and Michael J. Braddick, ed., *The British Atlantic World, 1500-1800* (New York: Palgrave, 2002); Christopher L. Brown, *Moral Capital: Foundations of British Abolitionism* (Chapel Hill: University of North Carolina Press, 2006); Bruce Dain, *A Hideous Monster of the Mind: American Race Theory in the Early Republic* (Cambridge, Mass.: Harvard University Press, 2002); Barbara J. Fields, "Slavery, Race and Ideology in the United States of America," *New Left Review* 181(1990): 85-118; Evelyn Brooks Higginbotham, "African-American Women's History and the Metalanguage of Race," *Signs* 17 (1992): 251-74; George Frederickson, *Racism: A Short History* (Princeton, N.J.: Princeton University Press, 2002); Winthrop Jordan, *White Over Black: American Attitudes Toward the Negro, 1550-1812* (Chapel Hill: University of North Carolina Press, 1968).

2. Orlando Patterson, *Slavery and Social Death: A Comparative Study* (Cambridge, Mass.: Harvard University Press, 1982), 13.

3. Aviam Soifer, "De Facto Slavery and the 'Syren Songs of Liberty and Equality': Carol Weisbrod, Much Obliged," *Connecticut Law Review* 40 (July 2008): 1317-1328. Several other historians have used the term "*de facto* slavery" in various contexts, see Edgar J. McManus, *Black Bondage in the North* (Syracuse, N.Y.: Syracuse University Press, 1973), 59; Margaret E. Newell, "Indian Slavery in Colonial New England," in *Indian Slavery in Colonial America*, Alan Gallay, ed. (Lincoln: University of Nebraska Press, 2009), 34; Paul Finkelman, *Slavery and the Founders: Race and Liberty in the Age of Jefferson* (1996; second edition, Armonk: M. E. Sharpe, 2001), 58; Stephen Middleton, ed., *The Black Laws in the Old Northwest: A Documentary History* (Westport, Conn.: Greenwood Press, 1993), 160, 272-73; for an opposing view on these states see John C. Hammond, *Slavery, Freedom, and Expansion in the Early American West* (Charlottesville: University of Virginia Press,

2007), especially 210; Maureen G. Elgersman, *Unyielding Spirits: Black Women and Slavery in Early Canada and Jamaica* (New York: Garland Publishing, 1999), 26, 34; Frank Mackey, *Done With Slavery: The Black Fact in Montreal, 1760-1840* (Montreal and Kingston: McGill-Queen's University Press, 2010), 28, 351; Emily West, *Family or Freedom: Free People of Color in the Antebellum South* (Lexington: University Press of Kentucky, 2012), 68-70, 112.

4. Kidd, *The Forging of Races*, 1-2.

ACKNOWLEDGMENTS

I owe an extraordinary debt of gratitude to the many scholars who have written about Afro-Vermont history. This book would not have been possible without the previous work of Gretchen Gerzina, Elise Guyette, Bill Hart, John Saillant, Jane Williamson, Kari Winter, Ray Zirblis, and many others. I am also deeply thankful to my colleagues Nick Muller, John Duffy, T.H. Breen, Sean Field, Bogac Ergene, Sean Stilwell, Jacqueline Carr, and Kari Winter, who read various drafts of this book. Specifically, I am indebted to Nick and John for sharing their deep knowledge of Vermont history. They saved me from making several silly errors of fact, omission, and interpretation. Sean Field patiently read every draft and offered important editorial advice. Kari kindly pushed me to broaden the context of my local history book, reminding me that Vermont slavery could be interesting to American historians outside of New England. The Vermont Historical Society's Publications and Research Committee, especially my editor, Alan Berolzheimer, and the reviewers, provided extensive constructive criticism that helped me rethink my evidence and interpretation. Alan stood behind this project and carefully offered the most insightful and helpful criticism. The wonderful staff at the Vermont State Archives, especially Scott Reilly and Mariessa Dobrick, helped me tremendously throughout the entire process of researching and writing the book. Jeffrey Marshall, Prudence Dougherty, Christopher Burns, and the staff at Special Collections of the University of Vermont library also provided invaluable advice and patiently helped with all of my requests. The librarians at the Vermont Historical Society, especially Paul Carnahan and Marjorie Strong, provided numerous documents for my study, ranging from bills of sale to obscure secondary sources. The Division of Reference, Law, and Information Services at the Vermont Department of Libraries in Montpelier also attempted to help me find various references. Joyce Higgins at the Charlestown Historical Society in New Hampshire generously shared information about Oliver Hastings and his relationship to Jotham White. The Town of Topsham kindly allowed me to use the John Barrett papers that included two important slave bills of sale. I also benefited from the work of the staff at the Bennington County Courthouse. Therese Corsones provided sage advice while helping me find certain Supreme Court cases in Rutland. I benefited tremendously from Judge Robert Mello's forthcoming biography of Moses Robinson. James Haaf and Judy Hayward provided important information about Dinah's early life. I would like to thank Carolyn Stone, whose early work on the failed 1791 Negro and Molatto Act helped me think about the implications of my own research. Lastly, Mark Stoler provided generous moral and financial support throughout the duration of this project and I am greatly indebted to him professionally and personally.

The Problem of Slavery
in Early Vermont

1777–1810

Introduction to the Study of Vermont Slavery

In 1786, the Vermont legislature proudly declared that "the Idea of Slavery is expressly and totally exploded from our free Government." Yet the very same law being described actually undermined the notion that slavery had been "exploded" from Vermont (see Document 11).[1] The law itself demonstrates that black people were reenslaved and sold to other areas after the promulgation of the 1777 Vermont Constitution, which granted freedom to slaves over ages 18 (women) and 21 (men) (see Document 2).[2] The history of abolition in Vermont is often cited as a positive story about slavery during the Revolutionary era, standing alone as a monument to early American emancipation. But the facts demonstrate a far more nuanced story of slavery and freedom in Vermont.[3]

This study makes several points about the complex history of Vermont slavery. The 1777 constitutional abolition of adult slavery did not end slavery or establish meaningful freedom for African Americans.[4] The legal reality of abolishing slavery did not always reflect social reality. The end of Vermont slavery was contested, contingent, complicated, and messy. Vermont made steps toward abolition, but slaveholding, kidnapping of free blacks, and child slavery continued until the early nineteenth century. Those who continued to own slaves were among the most respectable inhabitants of the state, ranging from Supreme Court judge and member of the legislature Stephen Jacob to the prosperous leading citizen of North Bennington, Moses Sage. It is difficult to assess the percentage or number of Vermonters who either owned slaves or supported slavery, but it is fair to state that they probably constituted a decreasing minority during the late eighteenth century. However, if the question is the percentage of Vermonters who supported fugitive slave laws or the exile of blacks out of individual towns for alleged misdeeds, then the numbers are higher, though probably still a minority. Two examples, discussed below, are the Bennington Friendly Society vote on returning slaves to their owners and the failed 1791 Negro and Molatto Act that garnered 31% of the legislative vote (see Documents 13 and 17).[5]

The point of this work is not simply to show that Vermont had slavery and denied equality to free blacks. For it is quite clear that slavery persisted after 1777 and free blacks struggled for meaningful citizenship. Nor is the intention to argue that slavery and racism are the dominant themes of Afro-Vermont history. Instead, the point here is to advance a more nuanced interpretation of local black history and race relations by including the story of slavery within the overarching themes of emancipation and freedom. The end of slavery must be viewed as a long process that occurred over thirty years (1777-1810), during which time emancipation, slavery, freedom, racism, hopes for natural rights, reenslavement, *de facto* slavery, and fleeting notions of black citizenship existed simultaneously (see Note on Terminology). This created a remarkable context for race relations whereby Afro-Vermonters could achieve freedom and some aspects of meaningful citizenship, but also faced the persistent threat of slavery, kidnapping, and the bondage of their children.

An examination of Vermont slavery elicits multiple questions about its nature, essence, and eventual abolition. How emancipatory was the abolition provision of 1777? Why did the framers write it in such vague terms? Why did Vermont forego enforcement provisions? How and why did slavery persist? Historian Raymond Zirblis aptly argues that "Vermont slavery, such as it is, dies a slow death" in the early 1800s.[6] More significantly, he points out that "the precise nature of servitude after 1777 remains unclear."[7] Therefore we need to understand the struggle between the forces of continued slavery and the movement toward freedom. These tensions in early Vermont beg for further study. Vermont historians can probe what the continuation of slavery in the state actually meant and how it affected free African Americans. The lives of free blacks in Vermont have benefited tremendously from the work of Gretchen Gerzina, Elise Guyette, John Saillant, Jane Williamson, and Kari Winter. Collectively, their work shows how Afro-Vermonters, such as Abijah and Lucy Prince, Jeffrey Brace, and Lemuel Haynes struggled and fought to enjoy the fruits of their freedom, but also did so within the shadow of slavery. They had triumphs and hardships, as exemplified by the Prince family, respectable farmers in Guilford, who used the court system to assert their rights, but also suffered from a mob attack on their property.[8] Black Vermonters always retained some agency in the making of their own lives and futures, but perhaps not under the most ideal circumstances.[9]

Without question, the Green Mountain State's 1777 abolition provision provided an essential foundation for the end of slavery in Vermont and other Northern states. It stands as an important monument to the slow legislative strangling of slavery in the North. Yet we can recognize the wonderful antislavery stories that percolate throughout the state's history while placing them alongside the story of slavery. In discussing slavery and its continuation, this need not deny the Bennington Church's resistance to their slaveholding pastor David Avery, or the glowing significance of Ebenezer Allen's decision in 1777 to free Dinah Mattis and her daughter Nancy because "it is not Right in the Sight of god to Keep Slaves" (see Document 3).[10] These examples provided black people with room to negotiate and advance their own freedom. From the time of the 1777 abolition provision (if not earlier), Afro-Vermonters challenged discrimination and attempted to give their children better opportunities than they had themselves.

The freedom of Afro-Vermonters as illustrated in the lives of free blacks in Hinesburgh and the individual stories of the Princes, Brace, and Haynes provide insight into the complicated and sometimes outright contradictory experiences African Americans regularly faced in Vermont. The presence of runaway slave advertisements, the lack of enforcement of the abolition laws, and the state convention's silence on joining a federal union that protected the slave trade, demanded the return of fugitive slaves, and gave the South extra representation for their slaves all expose the limitations and challenges to black freedom. Exploring Vermont slavery and its persistence allows us to fully consider the meanings of slavery, freedom, racism, and natural rights in the late eighteenth and early nineteenth centuries.[11] As James Wood Sweet argues, Northern abolition took place within the context of racist ideas and beliefs that remained ever present well after emancipation.[12] The problems facing free blacks throughout the Northern states confronted African-descended people in Vermont as well.

Although usually described by historians as an outlier or an exception to the broader trends of slavery in Revolutionary America, Vermont had some similarities to the troublesome history of abolition in other Northern states. This is not to deny some of the unique aspects of Vermont slavery, but from the use of Whig rhetoric about political enslavement to the support of the United States Constitution, the state's history of slavery and emancipation fits into the broader trends of Revolutionary history. Afro-Vermonters had opportunities not available in other parts of the Union. In theory, they could vote, serve in the militia, own property, and stand for election to state office. They could also give testimony in courts, bring lawsuits (sometimes winning these cases), and serve on juries. But, there was an important distinction between what blacks could legally do and the obstacles erected to block their exercise of citizenship rights. A crucial difference existed between the natural right as declared by the constitution of 1777 not to be enslaved and the political rights of citizenship. In the 1790s, some Vermont politicians tried to further circumscribe black freedom, return fugitives to slavery, and ban blacks from service in the militia (see Document 21). At the same time that some African Americans owned property, raised families, and attended churches, others suffered continued enslavement, kidnapping, and in some cases reenslavement.

The situation of slavery and problematic freedom in Vermont presents an extraordinarily complicated mosaic of race relations. In his remarkable study about Lemuel Haynes, John Saillant shows that several Vermont newspapers printed anti-slave trade and antislavery articles. Generally they condemned poor treatment of slaves, greedy slaveholders, and the difficult condition of well-meaning bondsmen and women.[13] That would not last, Saillant argues, because "many Vermonters of repute retreated from a vision of racial equality after 1810."[14] It seems clear that the advent of the Vermont Colonization Society in 1819 (the local auxiliary of the national American Colonization Society), the geographic and demographic expansion of slavery, and the evaporation of republican ideals and natural rights ideology resulted in increasing hostility toward African Americans.[15] The black population also increased in Vermont from 271 in 1790 to over 870 in 1830, years during which racism increased.[16] Saillant correctly states that hopes for racial equality became more remote after 1810, and that retreat can plausibly be connected to the persistence of slavery after 1777, the continued kidnapping and sale of black people, the implications of the attempted 1791 Negro and Molatto Act, and the lack of protection offered to fugitive slaves. The "vision of racial equality" resided more in the realm of theoretical natural rights than in concrete ideas and actions for black/white cooperation and understanding. The persistence of slavery and the roots of local racism occurred alongside of the successes of Lemuel Haynes and the Prince family. Opportunities for both black freedom and the persistence of slavery existed in the complex world of early Vermont.

TRIUMPHANT HISTORIOGRAPHY

Most historians accept that Vermont constitutionally or "immediately" abolished slavery in 1777. Numerous studies portray the state's abolition of slavery as an unproblematic triumph of emancipation. These works range from general studies about American and New World slavery to more focused volumes about the Founding Fathers or the Constitution. They assert that after 1777, slavery simply did not exist in the Green Mountain State. For example, in his wide-ranging study of slavery in North America, Ira Berlin mentions that Vermont "freed its slaves by constitutional amendment," primarily because slavery was economically insignificant and the black population small.[17] Peter Kolchin states that emancipation in Vermont "was immediate," noting that other states took a gradual route.[18] In *Inhuman Bondage*, David Brion Davis contends that "Vermont became the first region in the New World to outlaw slavery, in this instance by constitutional mandate."[19] In an earlier work, he wrote that the Vermont Constitution stands as unique because its assertion of natural rights led to prohibiting slavery. Davis also hits on a recurring theme throughout later literature—that "a zeal for liberty coincided with a small proportion of Negroes" living in Vermont.[20] Other historians mention the end of slavery in brief terms that may leave the inaccurate impression that little controversy or trouble underlay Vermont abolition. In his magisterial *White Over Black*, Winthrop Jordan simply notes that Vermont "banned slavery in its 1777 constitution."[21] Edgar McManus, in his seminal study, *Black Bondage in the North*, makes the same point.[22] Legal scholar Paul Finkelman refers to the abolition provision in the Vermont Constitution as an act of "absolute abolition."[23] David Waldstreicher states that Vermont "eliminated slavery."[24] In his indispensible edited collection, John Kaminski reprints the relevant section of the 1777 constitution outlawing slavery for adults.[25] More recently in *A Slaveholders' Union*, George Van Cleve comments that Vermont ended slavery for "persons of majority age."[26] In another recent study, the authors of the candidly titled *Complicity: How the North Promoted, Prolonged, and Profited From Slavery*, state that Vermont joined the United States "with a constitution outlawing slavery."[27] Finally, Antonio Bly's recent exemplary documentary history of runaway slaves in New England offers separate chapters for every state with the exception of Vermont. This is perhaps understandable given the book's detailed attention to Connecticut, Massachusetts, and Rhode Island—but it ignores the history of runaways and slavery in Vermont.[28] All of these accounts take Vermont's constitutional ban at face value, overlooking the deeper and more contested reality. The major reason for this oversight is that these books are about the broader trends of slavery and abolition in the United States and New World.

In this concentration on the larger story of Northern emancipation after the Revolutionary War, many historians do not examine the limitations on abolition in Vermont, much less the important 1786 Sale and Transportation Act, which clearly shows the continuation of slavery in the state (see Document 11). Further, they do not closely examine the vague wording of the 1777 constitutional ban on adult slavery, often ignoring its age-specific clause (see Document 2). Even Van Cleve's seminal work, which questions the depth and meaning of antislavery sentiment in the Northern states, surprisingly does not include an examination of slavery's persistence in Vermont, which would have in fact strengthened his claims about the weakness of antislavery legislation in the North.

General histories of the American Revolution and the early republic also observe Vermont's emancipation without treating its specific historical circumstance rigorously. In *Empire of Liberty*, for example, Gordon Wood cites the Vermont Constitution as an example of Americans' "increasing passion" to attack slavery.[29] Similarly, Norman Risjord points out the "growing sentiment" against slavery in the new nation and concludes simply that Vermont "prohibited slavery by its constitution of 1777."[30] Francis Cogliano's general history of revolutionary America also notes that Vermont "prohibited" slavery.[31] Francis Jennings ascribes Vermont banning slavery to the impracticality of plantations in the Green Mountain State, where "blacks were nonexistent."[32]

Two of the most important historians of the American Revolution, Bernard Bailyn and Wood, underestimate the role of slavery in the Revolution and the making of the United States Constitution. Instead, Bailyn argues that slavery had been "subjected to severe pressure" as the result of Revolutionary ideas.[33] Wood writes that the Revolution "set in motion ideological and social forces that doomed the institution of slavery in the North and led inexorably to the Civil War."[34] As Waldstreicher notes, "these historians (Bailyn and Wood) bring slavery back into the narrative as post-Revolutionary, *American* antislavery."[35] Thus, Vermont's abolition of slavery fits into a grand narrative of American abolitionism, true republicanism, and the happy result of the recognition of natural rights.

Although it is understandable that historians have wanted to place Vermont as an important and first link in the chain of Northern abolition, they have painted the state's emancipation history as reified and unproblematic. Too much emphasis on the emancipatory language of the constitution of 1777 has allowed other aspects of the state's history to escape. These accounts simply mention without investigating whether slavery had been fully abolished. They ignore the contingencies and complexities of Vermont's black history.

Some scholars, however, have taken a dimmer view of Vermont's antislavery activity. Generally speaking, they have highlighted the range of obstacles and opportunities facing African Americans in both Vermont and New England by acknowledging the role of slavery in the state's and region's history. In 1849, Daniel Chipman noted the existence of slavery in his biography of the state's first governor, Thomas Chittenden.[36] In *The First Emancipation*, published in 1967, Arthur Zilversmit noted that Vermont "explicitly outlawed slavery," but called the wording "somewhat vague" and open to interpretation as allowing slavery until men and women reached their respective majority. He argued that the constitution's framers wanted to forbid slavery, while allowing apprenticeships. Zilversmit recognizes some of the problems facing historians of slavery in Vermont, but he relied on secondary sources to construct his argument rather than investigating the constitution or the 1786 law.[37] John Saillant's 1993 book about Lemuel Haynes explored the possibilities and problems that Afro-Vermonters faced during the late eighteenth century. His careful research showed how Haynes dealt with racism and the vestiges of slavery.[38] Five years later, in *Disowning Slavery*, Joanne Pope Melish found that the language of the 1777 constitution "was sufficiently vague that slaveholding may have persisted without sanction in a few areas for several years."[39] In 2000, distinguished Vermont historian and bibliographer T. D. Seymour Bassett accurately argued that the Windsor constitutional convention hastily drafted its founding document and "left a loophole for minors to be held as slaves."[40] In 2005, Kari Winter's book *The Blind African Slave* showed the rich texture of black Vermont life through the personal life story of Jeffrey Brace, while also highlighting some of the startling obstacles he encountered.[41] Most recently, several historians including Zirblis and Guyette have shown that slavery and proslavery attitudes persisted in Vermont well into the nineteenth century.[42] These scholars have raised important questions, but historians must fully investigate Vermont slavery to find more satisfactory answers.

THE MEANING OF "SLAVERY" IN VERMONT POLITICAL DISCOURSE

Historians have long recognized how American patriots consistently used the general fear of political enslavement as an important rhetorical device for resistance to the British crown. For these patriots, enslavement meant absolute submission to an arbitrary authority and the loss of one's political will and self-determination. As Bailyn notes, this fear of slavery was not "simply lurid rhetoric" or hyperbole, but rather represented the very real and possible loss of personal autonomy and property.[43] Yet the claims of political slavery look rather hypocritical when compared with the stark reality of many of those same men denying freedom to the people they owned as slaves. The contrast between the Revolution's political ideals and the realities of American slavery eventually "became generally recognized."[44] This recognition had several consequences that did not necessarily produce antislavery or equalitarian outcomes. Instead, Revolutionary discourse contributed to negative views of African Americans. F. Nwabueze Okoye argues that the fear of political slavery represented a nightmare that the revolutionaries feared would befall them. More significantly, the use of the term "slavery" as a metaphor for the loss of political autonomy heightened the perceived differences between American patriots and their black slaves, making the possibility of racial equality even more remote.[45] Furthermore, the status of "slave" became almost the antithesis of virtue and autonomy. François Furstenberg shows that revolutionary political discourse resulted in whites blaming black people for their own enslavement because they lacked virtue; unlike the American revolutionaries, they did not adequately resist their own enslavement. In this tortured logic, white American political freedom and black chattel slavery were not contradictory.[46] As Jack Greene demonstrates, South Carolina patriots vehemently declared their great love of liberty precisely because they owned so many slaves.[47] Literary scholar Peter Dorsey shows how such rhetoric about slavery resulted in both advances for abolitionism and "the conservative reaction that took place after the war."[48] These excellent studies provide context for understanding how Vermont's political leadership and educated community used the word "slavery," what it meant, and how this discourse affected abolition and the future possibilities and opportunities for the state's black population.

Vermont leaders feared that New York, Congress, or Canada wished to subject them to a political "slavery." Ethan Allen and his supporters used inflammatory words like "slavery" or "enslaved" to fire up their supporters. They worried about the loss of political rights and the invalidation of their land titles. These anxieties resulted in Vermonters, especially the framers of the constitution, becoming increasingly hostile to various types of slavery, be it political threat or chattel. At the same time, some members of Vermont's political leadership held disparaging views of slaves that depicted them as the opposite of virtuous, honorable, and autonomous. These opinions made equality between blacks and whites unlikely, as local whites had been virtuous in defense of their rights, while African Americans had allegedly accepted their lowly place. In this view, slaves did not aspire to anything other than their next meal and simple amusements. Slaves were the antithesis of Vermont's tough backcountry population. White and black were as opposed to each other as "liberty is to slavery."[49] Black people, with slavish mentalities and character traits, could never share equality with virtuous white Vermonters. As a result, black pursuit of meaningful freedom immediately started off at an extreme disadvantage.

Ethan Allen provides a good example of this rhetorical dynamic. In 1772, he stated that the inhabitants of the New Hampshire Grants (the region that would become Vermont) must "defend themselves" against the "Cunning of New York." He concluded that New York had violated these citizens' natural rights and without fighting back they would "be by terms inslav'd."[50] Three year later, Allen addressed the New York Provincial Congress about the possibility of invading Canada and the success of the burgeoning American Revolution. He assiduously argued that the American colonies "must now sink to slavery, poverty, horrour, and bondage, or rise to unconquerable freedom, immense wealth, inexpressible felicity, and immortal fame."[51] Allen drew an extreme dichotomy between slavery and freedom, associating the horrors of slavery with people who did not "rise" to claim their freedom, "immortal fame," and economic independence. Those who resisted the British deserved freedom, while those who did not simply accepted slavery. In the realm of chattel slavery and black people in the Champlain Valley, this kind of rhetoric would fasten the chains of discrimination onto people who did not really deserve much better, having forfeited their own virtue and honor.

In 1779, Allen published his *Vindication*, a wide-ranging tract explaining Vermont's decision to form an independent state. It includes several metaphorical references to slavery as examples of what New York did to Vermont. Allen claimed that New York used its court system to force the people of the New Hampshire Grants to "yield up their property to [New York], and become their tenants and slaves."[52] In another section, grantees offered a cogent description of the enslavement that awaited them if they followed New York law: "If we submit in their execution of law, and become obedient and submissive subjects of their designing government," Allen argued, "we must soon yield to be their tenants and slaves; and we cannot see reason to conform to any law which will apparently bring us and our posterity into bondage, or manifestly deprive us of our property, but inasmuch as we boldly adhere to the maintenance of our property, which to us is very precious as it would be to the *New-Yorkers*."[53] To Allen slaves and slavery represented an utterly degraded state. The fear of political enslavement remained quite real for many people in the Grants. This association of slaves, and by extension black people, with such a debased and hapless condition only placed another brick in the wall dividing local whites and blacks. How could Vermonters view black people as fellow citizens? Afro-Vermonters lacking in virtue, courage, and honor, either deserved slavery or a condition barely better, but certainly nothing approaching citizenship. Thus, African Americans were exposed to racial discrimination that placed them on the margins of Vermont civil society. Historian Randolph Roth sums up this position accurately. "They were not recognized as equals by other Vermonters....blacks remained members of a servant caste in white eyes, and most opportunities were closed to them."[54]

Embedded in comments about slavery were other loaded terms that robbed virtue and honor from those who had become slaves. As Furstenberg points out, slavery became the fault of the enslaved in a no-win game of blaming the victim.[55] In 1785, Allen with typical flair wrote, "if we have not fortitude enough to face danger, in a good cause; we are cowards indeed, and must in consequence of it, be slaves....Liberty & Property or slavery and poverty; are now before us, and our Wisdom and fortitude, or Timidity and folly, must terminate the matter."[56] The traits Allen associated with slaves, including timidity and poverty, made them appear utterly devoid of every desirable human characteristic. Allen clearly asserted that possessing courage and virtue, one will not become enslaved, while those who lack honor and bravery will become slaves and deservedly so.

The stereotype of the indolent slave emerges in the writing of Ethan's troublesome brother, Levi Allen. Described by one historian as "the black sheep" of the family, Levi owned at least one slave.[57] He stated that the "indolent good natur'd slave can lay down and sleep provided his belly be full and meets with no disappointment if hunger doth not Overtake him, but to the Volitile ambitions be a death to be disappointed and a wound in his honor is infinitely worse than in his flesh."[58] Slaves were to be despised or laughed at for their laziness and "good natur'd" acceptance of their condition. They represented everything that free white Vermonters feared becoming if they were not adventurous, brave, virtuous, and honorable. As "A FREEMAN" wrote to the *Vermont Gazette*, there always remained the fear of falling into "those galling chains of slavery and despotism."[59]

The use of the word "slavery" in Vermont was both similar to and strikingly different from broader trends in American political discourse. Like their brethren, Vermonters associated their own enslavement with the loss of their political will and property. They saw it as an abhorrent imposition on their inherent liberties as Englishmen. But, a very significant difference between Vermont and the other American states lay with the real danger posed by New York, New Hampshire, and in 1777 the approaching British army, all of which threatened land titles in ways that residents of the Grants equated to slavery. Even after the defeat of John Burgoyne's army, Vermonters still feared political enslavement from New York, which would have entailed losing their political and land rights. Perhaps, more than in any other part of America, Vermonters acutely felt the prospect of political slavery to a neighboring state, which literally threatened to take away their property and some of their natural rights. Vermont needed to define itself not only as independent of New York, but as radically different. And paradoxically, part of this difference rested on outlawing slavery for black people of majority age—because denying the legitimacy of slavery made the Vermont backcountry different from New York, which permitted and prospered from slavery (New York had the largest slave population in the Northern states). Vermont's experience of possible political slavery at the hands of New York made continued chattel slavery problematic and contradictory to what the framers of its constitution thought of as natural rights. These natural rights, however, had some limitations.

THE PROBLEMATIC CONSTITUTION OF 1777

Vermont's declaration of natural rights, which legally outlawed adult slavery, demands intense examination. It does indeed stand as one of the first attempts in North America to undermine slavery. (Lord Dunmore's Proclamation of 1775 offering freedom to slaves of Patriot owners in Virginia predates the Vermont provision, but Vermont's action is the first legislative attempt at ending slavery in North America.) In the context of subsequent antislavery measures, in what ways was the Vermont Constitution exceptional? What did it share with gradual and/or immediate emancipation in other northern states?[60]

The culture of Vermont slavery and Vermont slave culture were similar to other forms of Northern bondage. Vermont slaves, like their counterparts in other New England states, had very close contact with their owners. Generally speaking, slaves and slave owners often lived in the same dwelling, ate together, socialized together, and worked alongside one another. Slaves would have labored in the same fields as their owners, tending the same animals, or inside the same artisan shop. Although this type of "family slavery" might foster kindness, it could also have been miserable for slaves who longed to leave their owners. Like slaves in other parts of New England, Vermont slaves worked in a mixed agricultural economy where they would have been engaged with the tedium of everyday farm tasks, from milking cows to helping plow to working the harvest. Surely, most of them would also have had various domestic responsibilities such as washing clothes, cleaning dishes, shoveling snow, clearing land, preparing firewood, making potash and pearl ash, and sweeping out the household. As most slaveholders only owned one or two slaves and the population of free African Americans was also small, enslaved blacks would have had the utmost difficulty in forming and developing families.[61]

Yet in certain ways Vermont was quite different. It did not have the same economic interest in slavery as other Northern states (Rhode Island, New York, Pennsylvania, and Massachusetts had much more capital and many more people invested in slavery and the slave trade), and Vermont had the smallest African American population. The number of Afro-Vermonters is difficult to determine before 1791 because of limited source material, but we can estimate some of the major population numbers and trends. Between

1770 and 1791, the black population in Vermont increased from around 25 to approximately 270. In 1770/1771, it is likely that most were slaves, but it is difficult to know what percentage remained enslaved in 1780, when perhaps 50 black people lived in the state.[62] Ray Zirblis suggests that during the colonial and early statehood eras, Vermont probably had about 65 to 70 slaves spread over numerous towns including Bennington, Windsor, Springfield, Manchester, Poultney, Hungerford (now Sheldon), Cabot, Burlington, Leicester, and Ferrisburgh.[63] He observes that the majority of slaveholders were well-to-do and that "typical owners were lawyers, doctors, ministers, businessmen and militia officers."[64] Zirblis further notes that the reason most Vermonters did not own slaves was the absence of ready cash to purchase them. He estimates that there were 33 slaveholders, which would mean masters usually owned only one or two slaves.[65] Thus, issues of slaveholder compensation and wild fears of miscegenation or racial intermixture did not hold the same place in Vermont's legislative decisions and political discourse as it did in other states.

Vermont also did not have an antislavery society until the 1830s (unless one includes the Vermont Colonization Society of the 1820s).[66] In contrast, Pennsylvania, Rhode Island, Connecticut, and New York had antislavery or anti-slave trade societies in the late eighteenth century. This is an essential distinction because these organizations usually attempted to protect black people from reenslavement, gave free blacks financial relief, and took legal action against recalcitrant masters.[67] Vermont did not have its Moses Brown, the wealthy Quaker merchant who eventually opposed the slave trade, or other wealthy benefactors willing to press for the freedom of kidnapped or reenslaved African Americans. This rendered Afro-Vermonters extraordinarily vulnerable.

The circumstances surrounding the writing of the Vermont Constitution and its ratification process make it unique. Several leaders of the New Hampshire Grants met at Windsor in June and again in July 1777, as General Burgoyne's invading army threatened the Grants. As historian Gary Aichele explains, Vermont had at least three political factions: the Allen group or Arlington Junto in the southwest; Jacob Bayley and the College Party in the upper Connecticut River Valley; and those who favored New York jurisdiction in the southeast, centered in Brattleboro and Guilford.[68] Despite these factions and the threat of the British army, the convention adopted a new constitution to protect the interests and independence of the Grants' settlers. Unlike the United States Constitution that followed a decade later, the Vermont Constitution explicitly uses the term "slave," and it appears twice. Largely copying the Pennsylvania Constitution, the first mention in the preamble blames the king for using "savages and slaves" against the American colonies. The second, more important mention of slavery came in the abolition provision after an explicit discussion of the meaning of natural rights.

> Therefore, no male person, born in this country, or brought from over sea, ought to be holden by law, to serve any person, as a servant, slave or apprentice, after he arrives to the age of twenty-one years, nor female, in like manner, after she arrives to the age of eighteen years, unless they are bound by their own consent, after they arrive at such age, or bound by law, for the payment of debts, damages, fines, costs, or the like (see Document 2).[69]

Why did the Vermont Constitution abolish adult slavery? What reasons lay behind the abolition provision? Randolph Roth speculates that the framers enacted the abolition provision to prevent "a labor-degrading, slaveowning aristocracy."[70] But it is nearly impossible to attribute motives to the Vermont founders or determine what the majority of Vermonters thought of the constitution, because records of the convention are scanty and it was not formally presented to the public for ratification. Historians do not know what motivated Vermont's leaders to adopt the abolition provision and any guesses would be speculation. However, there are aspects of the 1777 constitution that can be discussed in detail. The adult abolition provision contained several obvious loopholes, which allowed slavery to continue with little or no penalty at all. First, the vague language of this paragraph leaves its true intent unclear. In saying that no adult persons "ought" to be held as slaves, the framers used a nebulous and weak word. The word "ought" does not carry the same meaning as "shall" or another more declarative word or phrase.[71] The weakly worded Vermont provision does not for instance stand up to the 1780 Pennsylvania Gradual Abolition Act that declared: "all persons, as well as Negroes and Mulattos as others, who shall be born within this State, from and after the passing of this Act, shall not be deemed and considered as servants for life or slaves."[72] Those who drafted Vermont's constitution expressed more of a wish for than an actual prohibition of black bondage. In 1778, the government resolved "that a Committee of three be appointed, to prepare a bill, respecting the freedom of Slaves, agreeable to the bill of rights" (see Document 4).[73] The Assembly apparently understood that the constitution needed revision and clarification. Perhaps they planned to introduce enforcement mechanisms or prohibit child slavery. The committee might have considered banning the sale of slaves outside of the state. Unfortunately, the record remains silent on the details of this legislative attempt or perhaps the committee did not commence its work, as it never introduced a bill.

Outlawing slavery only for persons of majority age allowed slaveholding to continue throughout Vermont. The constitution allowed any slaveholder to continue to exploit young black children for up to twenty years in some cases. It should be noted that the scarcity of labor presented a problem in Vermont, and the use of apprenticeships or servitude could offer poor families a way to support children. Perhaps the toleration of slavery for black children until they reached majority age partially recognized that they would be poor and the framers expected them to be treated as apprentices, taught a trade, and gradually prepared for freedom. The allowance of child slavery might have been seen as a form of apprenticeship. Yet this rather positive view of the 1777 abolition provision does not deny the fact that the constitution gave slaveholders a form of compensation by which they could and did continue to exploit and benefit from black child and teenage labor. Permitting the continuation of child slavery meant black families could easily be separated, or freed parents could have felt obligated to remain on their masters' farms as inexpensive labor because they did not want to abandon children or younger relatives. Thus, Vermont's emancipation provision actually carried potentially devastating effects on black family and kinship networks.

The continuing existence of child slavery also provided slaveholders ample time to devise methods to sell their slaves to New Hampshire, New Jersey, New York, Québec, the Southern states, or the West Indies (see Document 14). Moreover, how could the Vermont authorities verify, even if they wished to, whether slaves had reached adulthood and should be free? A slaveholder could simply lie to authorities to buy more time before selling a slave out of the state. Without enforcement, the provision that slaves should achieve freedom upon reaching majority age remained moot. By offering nothing in terms of enforcing its antislavery provisions, the framers of the constitution allowed slavery to continue.

The Vermont founders did not offer any plans for the transition from slavery to freedom of the black population. African Americans' future economic and social opportunities received no attention. The founders and subsequent legislators exhibited little concern with the obvious change in social relationships that would take place between former slaves and their old masters. Moreover, the constitution said nothing about runaway slaves from other states and what Vermont officials would do about them. For example, would local authorities willingly help out-of-state owners in recovering their escaped slaves? Did New York slaveholders have the right to recapture runaway slaves who had escaped to Vermont? This clearly became the case after Vermont joined the Union in 1791. Moreover, the *Vermont Gazette* published several runaway slave advertisements from New York residents, one as early as 1786 (see Documents 12, 18-20, 22-25). In these various ways, the 1777 ban on adult slavery could easily be subverted, distorted, avoided, and totally disregarded.

Why did the framers write such a nebulous statement about slavery that had so many loopholes as to make it ineffectual in various ways? The vagueness of the Vermont abolition provision has two possible explanations. One is that the document was written in tremendous haste, with the fear of war and destruction on the horizon and inadequate time to consider the full implications of adult abolition. However, Vermont's political leaders did have the opportunity to reconsider and revise the adult abolition provision during the 1785 Council of Censors. The council recommended many changes to the constitution, but failed to address the inadequacies of the 1777 abolition law.[74] This lack of action suggests that they were satisfied with the constitutional wording as originally written. The second explanation is that Vermont's small black population and lack of extensive slaveholding simply did not demand thorough consideration of the issue. The framers may not have thought reenslavement or out-of-state sales would become problems. Also, they might not have considered that the doctrine of natural rights could be both liberating and extraordinarily limiting at the same time. As Winthrop Jordan states, the "only duty [natural rights] enjoined on government and men was negative—that they *not* violate the rights of other men."[75] In outlawing adult slavery, perhaps the Vermont founders thought they had done quite enough, and that newly freed black people needed to fend for themselves and recover or assert their own autonomy and virtue. Both explanations for the vague wording of the 1777 constitution were probably at work. The framers were rushed because of the British invasion and did not have time to fully and completely exchange ideas. More significantly, the small number of slaves and free blacks in their midst might have led the constitution's authors to not be overly concerned about the fate of African-descended people. The former slaves would have to take care of themselves, just like poor whites, especially those who had been indentured servants. After all, Vermont had no model for understanding the implications of ending slavery and what former slaves might need for economic maintenance and preparation for some form of citizenship.

The problems that beset Vermont abolition were far from exceptional in the experience of Northern emancipation legislation. Each Northern state faced similar difficulties of legal loopholes, compensation for slaveholders, lack of enforcement, racism, and the sale of black people out of state.[76] These intertwined issues reinforced one another. Northern states usually compensated slaveholders by giving them access to the children of slaves through indentured servitude or some other form of contracted labor that took away black children's liberty. For example, Pennsylvania's 1780 Gradual Abolition Act provided that slaveowners would be entitled to the service of slave children until they reached the age of 28.[77] Likewise, Rhode Island's Manumission Act allowed town councils to "bind out such children [those of slave mothers] as apprentices" until the ages of 21 and 18 respectively.[78] What is significant here is that the Rhode Island law specifically mentioned apprenticeships, while the Vermont abolition provision did not. As a result, black children in Vermont could remain slaves and also suffer sale outside of the state before 1786 (of course, they could be sold out of state illegally despite the Transportation and Sale Act). If Vermont had truly wanted the children of slaves to become apprentices, then the constitution would have said so explicitly. If that loophole was seen as an oversight, the Council of Censors could have corrected it in 1785, but they did not. The State of Vermont thus gave protections to human property and allowed child slavery to continue. By allowing slaveholders to retain children until adulthood, Vermont gave them a form of compensation. As Van Cleve concludes, "Northern abolition statutes took a very conservative approach, and provided slaveowners de facto compensation even for afterborn children by classifying such children as indentured servants and emancipating them only when they became adults (or even later)."[79]

Despite the admittedly sketchy evidence, we must grapple with two interrelated and essential questions. What motivated the founders to end adult slavery? What explains the ambiguous language of the abolition provision? These questions cannot be answered with any certitude. The founders were almost certainly motivated by natural rights philosophy, and they might have been inspired by religious ideals indicating that the enslavement of their fellow humans contradicted God's righteous intentions. Perhaps they hoped to prevent the development of a slaveholding elite who could monopolize capital or land. But natural rights ideology could actually be limiting rather than liberating. And perhaps the framers of Vermont's constitution thought that banning adult slavery would ensure that the black population would remain small and African Americans would not become a source of social or financial problems.

The constitutional prohibition of slavery is written in ambiguous terms that allowed for some forms of slavery, whatever the framers' true intentions. Without question, they rushed to finish their work in the shadow of the British army, and that may have resulted in a failure to fully consider the implications of their adult abolition provision. The vague wording is perhaps also a reflection of the framers' own uncertainty about what abolition actually meant. In taking such a momentous step, they were stepping far outside of what had been known in the British world. Perhaps freeing all slaves, especially young children, struck them as a potential financial drain, especially if townships ended up having to support indigent or abandoned children (towns would undoubtedly apply to the state to recover costs). As a result, they possibly considered it best for children to be left with their owners until they reached majority age. Of course, this left black children open to enormous abuses and we have one record of a boy under 10 being sold to New Hampshire and eventually out of the country (see Document 14). The framers were deeply invested in notions of private property and perhaps they wished to offer some form of compensation to slaveowners by allowing them to control black youth during some of their more productive years. We will never know with absolute certainty the reasons behind the abolition provision or its vague wording. But in Vermont, the end of slavery did not result in the establishment of meaningful freedom, as would also be the case in the British Caribbean and the United States in subsequent decades.

SLAVERY'S PERSISTENCE AND THE LIMITS OF ABOLITION: PROBATE RECORDS AND BILLS OF SALE

Vermont slavery continued for nearly thirty years after the advent of the state constitution. It persisted in two distinct ways. First, masters defied the law by purchasing and selling slaves. The limited evidence does not point to slaveholders exhibiting any sort of embarrassment in breaking the law. Indeed, those individuals who continued owning slaves included some of the most respectable citizens in the state, ranging from judges to military officers. Second, some white Vermonters styled African Americans as "servants," but this euphemism merely hid the fact that some of these people were either chattel or *de facto* slaves. As Guyette and Winter show, indentured black children lived in extraordinarily dangerous situations in a state that allowed child slavery.[80] They could easily be sold out of state before they reached majority age, which would have offered pecuniary benefits to their owners.

Slavery in Vermont did not usually attract the interest of the authorities. The open violation of the constitution and continued enslavement of African Americans was implicitly condoned. The scattered examples of slavery's open persistence can be found in bills of sale, probate records, court proceedings, church records, and town histories. These instances exist across the state, indicating that the widespread practice of continued enslavement was not confined to a single town or region of Vermont.

One of the most notorious and well-known examples occurred in Bennington. In 1780, David Avery moved to Bennington to become pastor at the Congregational church. He brought a female slave with him, which "created much dissatisfaction" in the church (see Document 6). One angry parishioner, Henry Walbridge, left the church because of its "scandalous" decision to allow Avery to serve as minister.[81] However, those who opposed his ownership of the woman "appear to have been in the minority."[82] Avery had other problems with his congregation, including his unwillingness to strictly follow the faith in his preaching, and by 1783 he had resigned and left town. At first glance this might seem a victory for antislavery residents, but Avery's resignation had more to do with religious issues than his slaveholding.[83] He openly owned his slave and had little or no interest in abiding by the law. Strikingly, Avery enjoyed the support of very important community members such as Jonas Fay, Isaac Tichenor, and Moses Robinson.[84] Jonas Fay served as a delegate to both constitutional conventions in 1777, so he certainly knew about the antislavery provision. Robinson later served as governor, senator, and state Supreme Court justice, while Tichenor would hold the governorship for many years in the late 1790s and early 1800s. Of course, these men knew that Avery owned a slave in defiance of the state constitution. Moses Robinson attempted to persuade Walbridge to return to the church but failed, and finally the church excommunicated Walbridge for his opposition to the slaveowning minister. Historian Robert Mello shows that Robinson's position as a church deacon influenced his decision that the unity of the church was more important than opposing Avery's slaveholding. Mello further points out that the "fact that Vermont's chief judicial officer, one of the authors of Vermont's Constitution, and other prominent Bennington leaders, proved willing to tolerate slavery" shows that some of the state's leaders were deeply ambivalent about racial attitudes.[85] It might be added that some of Vermont's political leadership were also quite ambivalent about ending slavery. They did not take the position of Henry Walbridge, despite the constitutional ban. Instead, they allowed slavery to continue in open defiance of the constitution. Perhaps the vague wording of the constitutional provision played out on the ground in Bennington, where Avery's slave certainly should have been free, but other issues took precedence. The local authorities did not seek to enforce the constitutional provision or do anything to Avery because of his slaveholding, nor did they act to free his female slave. Instead, local powerbrokers acquiesced in allowing Avery to hold a slave for the three years he remained in Bennington.

The complexities of gradual emancipation in Vermont can sometimes be discovered in the experience of one individual. During the late 1770s, Pompey Brakkee (or Pomp Brake) successfully challenged his enslavement in civil court. In the summer of 1778, Elijah Lovell (or Lovel) of Rockingham still owned Brakkee and according to Captain Leonard Spaulding, "pretended to have a bill of Sale of sd Pommp" (see Document 5).[86] Brakkee remained Lovell's slave well after the constitutional abolition provision, but eventually he challenged his bondage. We do not know how Brakkee found out about the abolition provision or why he waited for well over a year to file against Lovell. But in late spring 1779, Lovell failed to appear at court despite being called three times and the judges awarded Brakkee the surprisingly large sum of £400. As Robert Mello points out, "the record does not disclose exactly what Brakkee's complaint alleged," but it might have had to do with compensation for unpaid labor performed after 1777.[87] The case demonstrates that slavery persisted in Vermont, but also that it could be challenged by black people if they knew about the adult abolition provision and found a friendly court.

Brakkee's personal life history underlines the complexity of slavery's end in Vermont and raises many questions. The enactment of the constitution in 1777 did not immediately result in his freedom or that of countless others who might not have known about the constitution or been able to challenge recalcitrant owners in court. The questions we can ask about Pompey Brakkee are much more intriguing than the unsatisfactory answers the evidence allows. What did whites and blacks in Vermont actually know about the constitutional abolition provision? It is quite possible that certain segments of the population did not know about it, or that owners who did know attempted to hide it from their slaves. How did Lovell continue to enslave Pompey Brakkee after 1777, or to impose a form of bondage upon him that was like slavery? As Spaulding's account intimates, Lovell did not attempt to hide his ownership of Pompey and his neighbors certainly knew about it. Did one of Lovell's neighbors befriend Pompey and encourage him to file a civil court action, or did Brakkee find out himself and go directly to the court once he felt able to do so? Did this one slave's resistance encourage other local slaves also to resist? Although we do not know the number of black people living in Windham County in 1779, by the time of the first Vermont census in 1791 it had the largest black population of any county in Vermont. Pompey's brave resistance to his owner might have encouraged other slaves to find ways to escape from bondage. Even the little we know about Pompey Brakkee's story demonstrates that the abolition of slavery in Vermont must be approached with caution and an eye toward nuance. Although his case reveals that it was possible to force an end to slavery through the court system, other documentation and examples, ranging from legislative acts to probate records and bills of sale, tell the extent to which slavery continued after 1777.[88]

Several slaves appear in probate records and bills of sale after 1777, and this fact underlines the basic limitations of Vermont's abolition provision. In 1782,

John Armstrong died without writing a will. As a result, local commissioners divided his estate, real and moveable, among his relatives. One of Armstrong's valuable pieces of moveable property was "one Negro Boy" valued at £60 (see Document 7). The meaning of the word "Boy" is not clear. Given that black children in Vermont were seen as being worth less than adults because of the pecuniary costs of having to raise a child before she/he could provide valuable labor, it seems likely that the slave was not underage. The probate record does not record his name, age, or skill. However, the slave's price made him among the most valuable items of "property" on Armstrong's estate, which the commissioners valued at £1,648.[89] The estate's administrators noted that Armstrong's widow would inherit the slave. His fate remains unclear. The significance of the probate of Armstrong's estate goes beyond establishing the existence of slavery after 1777. It demonstrates that the commissioners, justice of the peace, and probate judge knew of Armstrong's ownership of a slave and included him as nothing more than moveable property in the probate record. The spirit of the 1777 abolition act ran into the realities of property ownership.

Vermont emancipation had further limitations, as several local bills of sale illustrate. In 1783, Samuel Andrew sold 14-year-old Rose to Colonel John Barrett (see Document 8). This young teenager probably faced continued slavery, as it would have made little sense for Barrett to free Rose four years after spending £22 to purchase her. Vermont's limited emancipation left young girls like Rose extremely vulnerable to remaining in slavery or easily being sold away.[90] During the same year, Jotham White sold Dinah to Stephen Jacob (see below, and Document 9).[91] Seven years later, Jotham White again flaunted the law by ignoring the 1786 Transportation and Sale Act. While serving as town representative for Springfield, White sold "my negro boy slave named Anthony, about eight years and a half of age" to Dr. Oliver Hastings of New Hampshire, where slavery continued to exist (see Document 14).[92] In that state, some officials and citizens believed that the 1783 constitution had ended slavery, but five years later the state Supreme Court's chief justice argued that slaves were not "Liberated by the Constitution or Laws of the State of New Hampshire."[93] He supported this interpretation by noting that the state Supreme Court rejected the case of a slave who had sued for wrongful imprisonment, claiming the constitution promised black people equality with their fellow white citizens. In 1790, there were over 150 slaves in the state and Anthony could easily have been held in bondage for many years in New Hampshire. In the bill of sale, White claimed that Hastings would have to free Anthony when the "slave" reached 21 years of age. How such a provision would be enforced is not clear. It is unlikely that anyone else would have seen the bill of sale, and it is unlikely that Hastings would have freed him simply based on that provision because he had paid the large sum of "thirty-five pounds in silver money" for the boy. Notarial records in Québec show that Hastings sold Anthony (Antoine) to Boucherville resident Charles Boucher de Labruere for 90 bushels of wheat.[94]

Another example of slaves being bought and sold is Jotham White's adult female slave named Dinah. When purchased by Stephen Jacob in 1783, Dinah was thirty years old, and she should have already been free, but instead she remained enslaved for at least another 17 years before her experience came to light as part of an 1802 Supreme Court case to recover from Jacob the cost of maintaining his property.[95]

23

DINAH'S STORY

Dinah's personal history suggests several of the intricacies and contradictions of slave life in Vermont (see Document 27). In 1783, Jotham White sold his "Negro Woman Slave, named Dinah, about thirty years of age" to Stephen Jacob of Windsor.[96] Historians know little of Dinah's early life: her place of birth (possibly Connecticut); how many times she had been sold prior to coming to Vermont; whether she had children or family nearby; the type of work she did. Historical documentation about female slaves, ranging from sexual exploitation to general patterns of life experience, can be limited.[97] The few details we have about Dinah's life are intriguing. According to the 1791 and 1800 censuses, she probably lived in Judge Jacob's household with another black person, but historians know nothing about this other person because of the limited information on these censuses.[98] Was this person a relative, a child, a husband, a friend, or another unrelated black person? The possibilities are tantalizing. We also know that local people considered Dinah an "excellent servant" and attempted to lure her away from Judge Jacob's household so she could work for them.[99] Dinah had a strong personality and refused to acquiesce to the demands of the town after Jacob's trial. In 1806 and 1807, Windsor's selectmen warned Dinah out of town, but she refused to leave and continued to board with different families. Local inhabitants eventually cared for Dinah during her final sickness and the town reimbursed them for their medical treatment of "Judge Jacob's Dinah."[100]

On the other hand, Stephen Jacob's life is well documented.[101] After attending Yale, he settled in Vermont in 1778 and began practicing law. Certainly he had read the state constitution and knew that it prohibited adult slavery. A man of ability, intelligence, and social standing, Jacob represented Windsor in the legislature and served on the Council of Censors in 1785. He also served on the Governor's Council and was actually sitting on the Supreme Court of Vermont during the time the selectmen of Windsor brought suit against him for costs incurred for taking care of his former slave.[102] Described as an "aristocratic" Federalist, Jacob continued to be a respected member of local society despite his blatant disregard for the law he had sworn to uphold.[103]

Dinah worked as Judge Jacob's slave for approximately 17 years from the end of the Revolutionary War in 1783. She probably performed numerous domestic tasks including washing clothes, cooking, cleaning, and yard work. According to the court record, Dinah "continued to live with and serve him as a slave until some time in the year 1800."[104] Although only 47 years of age, Dinah had become "infirm, sick, and blind." Jacob "discarded" Dinah and she became dependent on public charity, which had to pay for her "medicine," "support," and "attendance."[105] The selectmen of Windsor only brought suit when Dinah's freedom became a burden to the public treasury, not out of any sense of outrage that Judge Jacob had illegally enslaved her. Since the plaintiffs sought to recover damages incurred for caring for Dinah, they needed first to establish that she had been Jacob's slave. This did not seem to present a problem because they had a bill of sale. The court case shows the almost comical lengths to which the Vermont Supreme Court would go to deny the *de facto* existence of slavery by asserting its *de jure* illegality.

The crux of the case hinged on the plaintiffs' attempt to introduce Dinah's bill of sale into evidence. The defense attorney, Charles Marsh, objected to this request by arguing that "no person can be held in slavery in this State; and the showing of a bill of sale can be no evidence that the unfortunate being supposed to be transferred by it as a human chattel, is a slave."[106] He concluded that the bill of sale was void because of the first article of the 1777 Vermont Constitution. Judge Jacob's counsel further argued that his client could not bear responsibility for the money spent by the town because slavery did not exist in Vermont; this despite the authenticity of the bill of sale and the fact that the court and community knew that Jacob had held Dinah as a slave. The attorney for the plaintiff attacked this reasoning because it excused Vermont slaveholders, who continued to flaunt the law, from any sort of responsibility for their black servants or slaves who could be turned out of the house when no longer useful. The plaintiff's counsel, Jonathan Hubbard, highlighted the continuation of slavery in Vermont as late as 1800 and the dangers of ignoring it. He argued that though "no person can hold a slave *de jure* by our constitution, yet there may exist among us a slave *de facto*." He also shifted to higher ground: "[t]hat if a master will hold an *African* in bondage as a slave, contrary to right, and for a succession of years, during which the slave *de facto* spends the vigour of her life in his service, and in which she may be presumed to have earned for the master sufficient to maintain her in the decrepitude of old age, there is a moral obligation upon the master to support her when incapable of labour."[107] He further argued that the laws of the United States, which acknowledged slavery, held sway in Vermont and thus the bill of sale should be admitted as evidence.

Marsh offered a weak, but effective rebuttal. According to him, Judge Jacob had brought Dinah into Vermont and "there can be but little doubt, from the excellent character and disposition of her master, she would have so continued until this time in sickness and in health."[108] He accused the selectmen and others of enticing Dinah away from Judge Jacob. Marsh recounted that, "discovering that she was an excellent servant, and wishing to profit themselves of her labours, [they] inveigled her from her master's family and service by the syren songs of *liberty and equality*, which have too often turned wiser heads."[109] Marsh asserted that they had "wasted her strength in their service" and she became blind and paralyzed. As a result, he denied that Judge Jacob could be held responsible for her maintenance. In an argument of amazing hypocrisy, Judge Jacob's counsel claimed that his client did not attempt to retrieve his slave "in obedience to the constitution" because Jacob believed he could not legally hold her as a slave. This in spite of the fact that he had done so for the better part of two decades! Jacob denied that he should be responsible for maintaining Dinah and that the best way to deal with the situation would be to warn her out of town. Jacob clearly felt little concern for Dinah despite the excellent service she had rendered him for so long. His attorney concluded that the real question hinged on whether "the defendant [was] obligated to refund moneys advanced by others" for the care of his former slave in a state where the principle of slavery "cannot be admitted."[110]

The assistant judge, Royall Tyler, argued that the Vermont Constitution strictly outlawed slavery and that the Federal Constitution did not affect this particular case. He thus objected to the bill of sale being introduced as evidence. He seemed to take very little notice of Hubbard's argument about the *de facto* continuation of slavery in the state. Tyler preferred to adhere to the wording of the constitution of 1777 rather than to examples of how this provision had been ignored, subverted, and contradicted. The chief judge (Jonathan Robinson) agreed with his assistant, declaring that "when the question of slavery involves solely the interests of the inhabitants of this State, I shall cheerfully carry into effect the enlightened principles of our State Constitution."[111] As a result, he did not allow the bill of sale into evidence, which nonsuited the plaintiffs.

Dinah's case has several points of significance for the study of Vermont slavery. It seems that the residents of Windsor accepted Jacob's slaveholding. They knew of the enslavement of this woman.[112] The court case itself showed the willingness of the justices to accept a legal fiction that slavery did not exist because the state constitution banned it, while ignoring the reality of slaveholding. The judges certainly knew that their fellow justice had a slave in his household. They seemed unwilling to admit that one of their own had so brazenly broken the law and defied the constitution. Just as disturbing, the court indicated that slaveholders did not owe their manumitted ex-slaves any support or sustenance even though they had spent their lives laboring for an individual or family. The court papers also reveal that some forms of slavery would be accepted in Vermont as part of the *lex loci* of another state. However, once an individual with slaves became an inhabitant of Vermont, his or her bill of sale proving ownership would cease to operate. This allowed slaveholder sojourns in Vermont, and without proper enforcement people could continue to exploit and own slaves until authorities intervened.[113] Dinah's case demonstrates that slavery persisted in the open and among the most respectable citizens. It also shows that when Dinah refused to accept the town's attempt to warn her out, the selectmen had to care for her in her final days. In this sense, she successfully claimed the right to have her medical and other expenses covered by the town where she had served one of its most eminent residents.

PATTERNS AND QUESTIONS IN TOWN HISTORIES
AND CENSUS RECORDS

Dinah's sad saga of slavery is not an isolated incident, as several other examples of slaves being held openly in Vermont demonstrate. Levi Allen owned a "Negro fellow Prince" whom he had purchased from Jacob Lansingh in New York (see Document 10). Allen had spent part of the war years serving the Loyalist cause and participated in land speculation in the slave societies of East Florida and South Carolina. During the 1780s, Levi owned Prince, who suffered from an eye problem, in Vermont and trusted him to perform "commercially valuable tasks."[114] Prince later settled in Windsor and applied for a military pension and noted his eye issues, which he attributed to a war wound. Ethan Allen also had a few black "servants," but their actual legal status remains unclear, and they may have been slaves at some point during their residence in Vermont.[115] Others also openly flaunted the constitutional ban. In Springfield, Lewis Morris brought several slaves to work on his farm in the mid-1780s. Eventually, the antislavery sentiment of some residents "caused some embarrassment to General Morris," which resulted in "a change in status of some of his entourage [Morris's slaves gained their freedom]."[116] In 1790, General Platt Rogers purchased land in Basin Harbor. He brought slaves from his New York home to his new property in Vermont. Rogers's slaves gained their freedom, and he gave them land that became locally known as "the Negro Orchard."[117]

During the same year, Colonel Elisha Sheldon's son George and "several Negro servants" came to land Sheldon owned in northern Vermont near the Québec border. These black servants, very likely slaves, helped their owners with the harvest. By the late spring Colonel Sheldon, his other sons, and "their Negro servants" had settled in this frontier town, which they named Sheldon. Coming from Litchfield County, Connecticut, the Sheldon family had experience with slavery, and it seems unlikely that their "Negro servants" were actually free blacks who decided on their own volition to travel to the Vermont backcountry.[118] In the census of 1790, Connecticut listed 2,648 African American slaves and 2,271 free blacks; those slaves comprised 70% of all the slaves reported in New England.[119] The Sheldon family held slaves in Connecticut and most likely brought them as slaves to Vermont. The first child born in the town "was a colored child; its mother, 'Old Mary' was a servant of Col. Sheldon, who purchased her in Connecticut where she was sold for the commission of some crime."[120]

In 1800, 23 years after the 1777 constitutional ban on slavery, Captain Moses Sage "owned one Negro slave" in North Bennington. Described as the "aristocrat of the village," Sage owned a sawmill, clothing shop, and general store. Thus, one of the most respectable citizens of this little village had no problem flaunting his wealth by possessing a slave in direct violation of the constitution.[121] Perhaps the latest example of open slaveholding in Vermont is found in the 1810 census, where two Vermont men, one in Salisbury and the other in Leicester, owned slaves (see Document 31).[122]

Thus, despite the 1777 abolition of adult slavery, examples of slaves in Vermont ten to twenty years after the constitutional prohibition are clearly documented in town histories. Some of the most respectable and well-to-do residents of the state engaged in slaveholding. Moses Sage, Platt Rogers, and the Sheldon family held positions of importance in their respective towns and villages. The choice they made to hold slaves made a mockery of the constitutional abolition of slavery. The public nature of slaveholding by respectable members of the community after the 1777 ban demonstrates some level of local acquiescence. In the small town of North Bennington, most residents would have known that the wealthiest resident, Moses Sage, owned a slave, just as the inhabitants of Sheldon would have known that its founding family kept slaves. Residents of Windsor probably were aware of Dinah's presence in Stephen Jacob's household, and probably believed her to be held in bondage; members of the selectboard definitely knew of her status. Slavery persisted in the open and remained sanctioned by some local elites throughout the late eighteenth century. This reality does not deny that Vermont's state government took an important step toward emancipation, but it makes clear that the vestiges of slavery continued. The line between slavery and freedom was complicated and contested.[123]

Census evidence suggests a similar picture. The first census of Vermont, published in 1791, originally recorded "16 slaves in Vermont."[124] In 1870, the chief clerk of the Census Bureau, Vermonter George Harrington, discovered that there had been an oversight in the enumeration of the black population.[125] According to the Census Bureau, the "original error occurred in preparing the results for publication, when 16 persons, returned as 'Free colored,' were classified as 'Slave,'" claiming there "never were any slaves in Vermont." It seems that Harrington and the Census Bureau had determined not to find any Vermont slaves rather than carefully investigating the nebulous status of blacks in the Green Mountain State.[126] The simple but problematic categories of "slave" and "all other free persons"—by which the census meant free blacks, Native Americans, and people identified as "mulatto"—deny the gray area in which many black Vermonters found themselves. A close examination of the 1791 and 1800 censuses reveals several examples of black people living in white households who could have been slaves (see Document 15). The census records also show black people listed as free in various white households known from other sources to have owned slaves. In Vermont, the difference between slave and servant remained blurry. Kari Winter points out "some census takers felt that 'free coloreds' were *de facto* slaves or that 'black' and 'slave' were interchangeable terms."[127]

The 1791 Vermont census reveals that only a few white households had four or more African Americans living with them. Indeed, it was rare for any white household in Vermont to have more than one African American domestic or farm hand living with an individual family. The limitations of the 1791 census, including undercounting slaves and the lack of information about gender or age, renders it nearly impossible to determine or understand the relationships between African Americans within these households (see Document 15). For example, Jonathan Fisk's Bennington home included four African Americans, but no records exist that allow us to determine their relationships to one another.[128] Did these four make up some type of family? How did they end up in this one man's household? And, of course, the most significant question, why did four black people live in this white household?

Possibly they were indentured servants, farm laborers, domestics, or perhaps they were slaves. In Windham County, the 1791 census recorded 58 African Americans, the most of any county.[129] The households of John Stroud in Dummerston, Henry Cole in Brattleboro, and Nathaniel Foster in Putney included 10 African Americans each. The census listed all of these people as "free." In Ferrisburgh, in Addison County, 9 African Americans resided in Jonathan Saxton's household.[130] It seems unlikely that any white-headed household in Vermont would have contained 9 or 10 free African Americans. Why did any of these households have so many black people in them? Were they indentured servants, free laborers, or slaves? Did African American families live in any of the households? How many of these people were children? Perhaps these white families offered generous laboring terms and allowed black families, who would have been otherwise broken up, to stay together. But these African Americans also could have been slaves or unfree laborers. According to the 1800 census, the households of Saxton, Cole, and Foster no longer recorded any African American residents, and John Stroud appears to have left the state.[131] What happened to the black people in these households during the 1790s? They could have moved and became independent householders; but Saxton, Cole, or Foster might also have sold them as slaves out of the state.

Taken together, these examples raise many questions about the status of black people in late-eighteenth-century Vermont. They also open up questions about the nature of black/white relations, how they were formed, and what they meant. How did 10 black people come to live in a white family's household? From where did they come? Were they slaves or former family slaves brought to Vermont from elsewhere? Although the 1791 census lists these African Americans as free, that classification might be due to the discomfort of local white people who continued to struggle through the process and meaning of illegal adult slavery and the difficulties of abolition (see Document 15). It probably obscures the continued reality of coerced labor and unfreedom imposed on Afro-Vermonters.

For some cases in which the 1791 and 1800 censuses listed white families as having free blacks living in their households, other evidence reveals that they were in fact slaves. The case of Judge Stephen Jacob, who owned Dinah, provides the most obvious example. In both the 1791 and 1800 censuses, Jacob's household was recorded as including two free African Americans. In reality, one of these people trapped in the Jacob household was the enslaved Dinah, as disclosed in the court records. Yet the census enumerators denied the existence of slavery in Windsor.[132] In 1783, John Barrett purchased a young teenage girl named Rose in Springfield, Vermont, for £22 (see Document 8). The 1791 census recorded two "free" African Americans in Barrett's household, and it seems likely that Rose was one of these two.[133] Barrett had also purchased an African American woman in 1770 (see Document 1), and according to folklorist Mary Eva Baker, this woman (also named Rose) "lived and served him [for] many years."[134] One last example is Moses Sage, the "aristocrat" of the little village of North Bennington. In 1800, one local observer noted that he possessed a slave. The 1800 census confirms that one black person lived in his household, but listed this person as free.[135] The evidence is contradictory. These examples highlight the ways in which slavery persisted in the shadows of the official records and lurked behind linguistic euphemisms. The opposed categories of "free" and "slave" probably do not capture the actual status of some blacks in post-Revolutionary Vermont, whose everyday life experience might not have reflected their legal or census designation as "free."

THE LIMITATIONS OF THE 1786 LAW

The reason slavery continued in Northern states was that abolition laws contained immense loopholes and practically no enforcement mechanisms. The Vermont Constitution provides an excellent example of abolition declared by law but lacking accompanying enforcement provisions for nearly a decade. To be fair, the Vermont Constitution itself contains no enforcement language for any of its decrees. So the absence of accompanying measures to enforce the abolition of adult slavery is not surprising. However, between 1777 and the fall of 1786, Vermont's legislators did not create any enforcement mechanisms, appropriate any funds to oversee an orderly end to slavery, or impose fines on those who broke the law. The assembly could have enacted such laws through the 1778 committee on slavery or the 1785 Council of Censors, but no legislation was considered until the 1786 Sale and Transportation Act, and even this law had several limitations.

The Sale and Transportation Act underlines the continuation of slavery and the kidnapping of free blacks for nearly a decade after the passing of the original provision for abolition in 1777 (see Document 11). It took Vermont legislators nine years to correct this hole in the constitutional provision. Rhode Island had banned out-of-state slave sales in 1779, but Vermont would wait seven more years to deal with this very same issue. The 1786 law provides *prima facie* evidence of the existence of slavery in Vermont and the determination of the legislature to block further sales and kidnappings of African Americans. The wording of the law explicitly expresses the realities of local slavery, the hope for a state free of slavery, and a new determination to stop out-of-state sales. Ray Zirblis postulates that Vermonter William Ward's purchase and subsequent sale of four New York slaves to Montreal, including an infant, led to the Sale and Transportation Act.[136] In any case, the wording of the statute is striking:

> Whereas by the Constitution of this State all the subjects of this Commonwealth of whatever colour are equally entitled to the in-estimable blessings of Freedom unless they have forfeited the same by the commission of some crime, and the Idea of Slavery is express-ly and totally exploded from our free Government.
>
> And whereas Instances have happened of the former owners of Negroes in this Commonwealth making sale of such persons as Slaves notwithstanding their being liberated by the Constitution, and attempts have been made to transport such persons to foreign parts in open violation of the Laws of the Land.
>
> Be it therefore enacted by the General Assembly of the State of Vermont that if any person shall hereafter make sale of any subject of this State or shall convey or attempt to convey any subject out of this State with intent to hold or sell such person as a Slave every person so offending and convicted thereof shall forfeit and pay to the person injured for such offence the sum of £100 and cost of suit to be recovered by action of debt complaint or Information.[137]

The first paragraph made two significant points. First, it claimed that all people, including African Americans, were entitled to the freedom offered by the commonwealth, echoing the high-minded rhetoric of the constitution. Yet this assertion of freedom for all its citizens reflected more hope than reality, because the second assertion, that slavery was "totally exploded" from Vermont's "free" government, was obviously not true or else this law would not be necessary. Vermont could not claim to be thoroughly antislavery when its practices had opened the door to continued slavery, and when the constitution continued to permit child slavery whether or not the intention had been to promote apprenticeships. Theoretically, the government rejected the idea of slavery, but the reality was more problematic.

The second part of the law explicitly recognized the vestiges of slavery in Vermont. The language is clear that it responded to the so-called "former owners of Negroes" selling slaves out of the state. In other words, enough "Instances" of the sale of black people to other areas must have occurred to get the attention of the assembly and result in the passage of the law. Slavery clearly had not ended for adult African Americans and certainly not for their still-enslaved children who had not reached the age of majority spelled out in the constitution. Some people continued to use the confusion of the law and the state's failure to enforce its own antislavery provisions to sell recently freed black people to slaveholding states.

Despite the intention to enforce the abolition mandate, however, this new statute had clear limitations. The 1786 law did not address the sale of slaves within Vermont, or instances of intrastate kidnapping whereby local whites reenslaved blacks within the state's borders. It also did not address the question of child slaves and whether or not they could be sold out of the state, since they were still legally enslaved or under indenture. Also, Vermont slaveholders could clearly move with their slaves to another state or give such slaves to another family member who moved out of state, to avoid having to forfeit their investment when those slaves reached majority age. Nor did the law explain how suits would be brought to court and prosecuted. The question remained open about how the state could garner enough evidence to convict someone of the offense of sale and transportation. Despite the potential advances in enforcement, several questions and possible loopholes remained.

Vermont's 1786 act mirrored the steps taken by other Northern states to prevent reenslavement and transportation to the Southern states or the West Indies. The problems and circumstances surrounding similar laws in other Northern states mirrored some of the issues faced by Vermont. In Pennsylvania, eight years elapsed between the adoption of the gradual abolition act in 1780 and the advent of legislation to prevent the "removing or selling [of] slaves out of the state."[138] Yet Vermont and Pennsylvania differed in other significant ways. The Pennsylvania Abolition Society brought several cases against those accused of wrongful enslavement or selling slaves to another region. This well-funded and active organization "was responsible for protecting hundreds of African Americans against slavery or reenslavement over several decades."[139] Afro-Vermonters did not benefit from any similar organization. Massachusetts and Connecticut also passed legislation to prohibit out-of-state sales of African Americans. Like the Vermont legislation, both laws contained large loopholes that suggest they permitted some forms of slavery. In Massachusetts, the lack of clarity regarding the actual end of slavery resulted in the state not banning kidnapping until 1785. In 1788, Massachusetts prohibited participation in the slave trade and also permitted prosecution against those caught reenslaving and attempting to sell such captives out of the state. In these two states, along with Vermont, kidnapping and out-of-state slave sales continued well after the legal prohibition against such sales. The underlying problem remained one of enforcement.[140]

Thus, slaveholders and others had evaded Vermont's 1777 constitutional ban on adult slavery and the legislature had admitted as much by enacting the 1786 Sale and Transportation Act. As George Van Cleve points out, for these types of sales and kidnappings to persist there had to be some "minority" support for the removal of blacks as part of the process of abolition.[141] It is fair to note that a minority of Vermonters violated the constitution's abolition provision. But the process of emancipation in Vermont remained difficult and contingent. Twenty years later, in 1806, Vermont passed an Anti-Kidnapping Act because the reenslavement and sale of black people out of the state had clearly continued after 1786 (see Document 30).

VERMONT, SLAVERY, AND THE FEDERAL UNION OF 1791

Three interrelated episodes—the 1791 union with the United States, the attempted repeal of the 1786 Act, and the corresponding failure to protect fugitive slaves—underline the limits of abolitionism and the persistence of slavery in Vermont. The small republic debated joining the Union at a convention in the first month of 1791. Delegates discussed numerous benefits of and problems with joining the United States. The vast majority (over 95% of the participants) supported and approved of Vermont statehood and accepting the United States Constitution. However, a few voices were in dissent. These local "Anti-Federalists," such as Daniel Buck of Norwich, feared that if Vermont entered the Union "her interest must then bend to the interest of the union."[142] Perhaps they were concerned about the issue of slavery, but it is hard to tell, for the convention did not choose to address any aspects of slavery or the slave trade. The delegates seemed unconcerned about how Vermont's abolition provision conflicted with the United States Constitution's fugitive slave clause. To understand Vermont attitudes about the slave trade, fugitive slave clause, and three-fifths ratio, historians must look beyond the uninformative convention notes to other sources and subsequent events to unearth Vermont politicians' views about these critical constitutional issues.

The majority of Vermonters probably opposed the slave trade, even though they did not address any contradiction in adopting the U.S. Constitution while holding onto their anti-slave trade ideals. For example, celebrating the Fourth of July in 1792, residents of Windsor toasted President Washington, Congress, and "The British Nation—May their Philanthropy in the abolition of the Slave Trade, be imitated by all Nations."[143] National Federalists regularly painted the possible 1808 end of the trade as a vast improvement over the Articles of Confederation, under which they said the trade could have gone on forever.[144] In the early nineteenth century, Vermont's Assembly backed any federal laws that would end the slave trade. Supporting such a constitutional amendment, Governor Isaac Tichenor called on the Assembly for its best efforts to "repress that impious and immoral traffic."[145] The Assembly agreed and required that the state's congressional delegates take every possible measure to quickly pass an amendment to prevent the "further importation of slaves, or people of colour, from any of the West India islands, from the coast of Africa or elsewhere into the United States" (see Document 29.[146] Embedded in this denunciation of the slave trade is an explicit wish to ban immigration of "people of colour." The desire to end the slave trade developed alongside general doubts that black people could usefully fit into the social fabric of Vermont or New England.[147] As Joanne Pope Melish explains, many white New Englanders associated black people with idleness, poverty, and potential social disorder.[148] Most white Vermonters had limited contact with African Americans and they simply could not imagine how increasing numbers of free blacks could live in their communities and coexist. In these debates, 14 years after joining the Union, Vermont strongly condemned the slave trade, even as it avoided questioning domestic slavery or offending the South, and even as strong ambivalence about or distaste for black people in its midst was put on full display.

Vermont politicians probably held split ideals on domestic slavery, which ranged from keeping the South and its Northern shipping allies happy to criticizing the counting of slaves for any purposes of representation. Events demonstrate that Vermonters placed the political demands of Southern states above any moral scruples regarding the federal ratio or slavery. In 1804, the Massachusetts legislature asked Vermont to join them in adopting a resolution to exclude slaves from the apportionment of congressional representatives.[149] The authors of this proposition thundered that the three-fifths ratio was "unjust and injurious….a planter possessing fifty slaves may be considered as having thirty votes, while a farmer in Massachusetts, having equal or greater property, is confined to a single vote." They feared becoming further marginalized because of the Louisiana Purchase, which would "destroy the real influence of the Eastern States in the National Government."[150] The Massachusetts legislators saw Vermont as a natural ally against the Southern beneficiaries of the three-fifths clause. Vermont's Assembly, however, refused (105 to 65) to support the initiative, fearing the wrath of the Southern states and further disunity throughout the country (see Document 28). "The amendment proposed, as we conceive, would materially affect a part of the federal constitution which was in fact the result of a spirit of compromise, and which guarantees to some states in the Union, a right, which to them is

sacred; a right, in consideration of which mutual benefits are secured to us."
In this sense, Vermont upheld Southern power in congressional representation and the Electoral College. The Assembly concluded that "the amendment
proposed would have a tendency to destroy, rather than confirm, that union
among the several states, so essential to our national prosperity."[151] Given Vermont's willingness to acquiesce to the three-fifths ratio, it is not surprising
that state legislators attempted to pass draconian legislation designed to repeal the 1786 Sale and Transportation Act.

THE SIGNIFICANCE OF A FAILED LAW:
THE 1791 NEGRO AND MOLATTO ACT

35

 The 1791 Negro and Molatto Act attempted to circumscribe black freedom
and reenslave runaway fugitives (see Document 17). Its supporters wanted to
repeal the 1786 law, allow for the indenture of allegedly "idle" black people,
and encourage Vermonters to participate in hunting down and turning in
fugitive slaves to out-of-state masters. The proposed act attempted to restrict
the freedom of Afro-Vermonters, while ensuring that black people from out of
state were either returned to their previous condition of servitude or heavily
monitored if allowed to remain in the Green Mountain State.[152] The act failed
by a vote of 59 to 27 and was referred to the next session, but the Assembly did
not revisit the legislation. Legislators did not discuss the law again because,
as Judge Royall Tyler noted in his 1802 decision about Dinah, "upon our admission to the Federal Union, the statute laws of this State were revised, and
a penal act [the 1786 Transportation and Sale Act], which was supposed to
militate against the third member of the 2d section of the 4th article of the
constitution of the *United States* [the fugitive slave clause], was repealed" (see
Document 27).[153]

The introduction to the proposed legislation reveals the true nature of
the act. It reads, "A Bill, entitled, An Act to enable the masters of slave[s] or
servants who escape from them, to apprehend such slaves and servants, and
carry them out of this state and to enable the selectmen of the several towns
of this state to bind out to service such free negroes as appear to them indolent, vicious or likely to become chargeable to the public."[154] The intention of
this proposed law was two-fold: to return runaway slaves who might become
public charges by sending them back to slavery, and to indenture local blacks
who were allegedly "indolent" and transient. The authors of the law wanted to
limit opportunities for fugitive slaves to hide in Vermont, but they also wanted

to control the freedom of movement of black people by regulating their labor through a system of indentures that could easily have become abusive and exploitative.

It is possible to create a brief profile of the lawmakers who supported this proposed legislation. The bill's major supporters included Judge Elijah Paine (Orange County), Judge Lemuel Chipman (Rutland County), and Stephen R. Bradley (Windham County), who all served on a committee to prepare the legislation for a formal vote.[155] Every county, with the exception of Bennington, had at least one representative who voted for the 1791 Negro and Mulatto Act.[156] Although only 23 African Americans resided in Chittenden County in 1791, 5 state legislators representing towns in the county voted to support the bill. Perhaps they feared an influx of fugitive slaves from New York or Canada who might become public charges. The county with the largest black population—Windham with 58—had only had two state legislators who supported it. Orange and Rutland Counties had 5 and 4 supporters of the proposed legislation, respectively. The Negro and Molatto Act drew its greatest number of supporters from Windsor County—the place where Vermont slavery persisted the longest—where 8 representatives voted for it, including Jotham White, the same person who was behind two slave bills of sale in 1783 and 1790. Although the bill failed, approximately 31 percent of the members of the Assembly voted for it, indicating that a substantial minority of Vermont lawmakers supported legislation that would have denied blacks the basic benefits of freedom, while encouraging slavery and the sale of blacks out of state.[157] As Carolyn Stone's work demonstrates, Vermont legislators introduced the bill out of deeply fearful sentiments about increasing numbers of idle, indolent, and poor vagrants.[158] Perhaps it garnered support because of a deep-seated Yankee frugality that feared public expenditures on an unwanted segment of the population, which struck certain lawmakers as wasteful.

The care of an indigent person of African descent in Rutland served as the moving force behind the 1791 legislation. In early 1789, John Johnson, a former soldier of the French Army in the United States, arrived in Rutland with "Ten or Twelve Lerge Runing Sores between his Knee & his hip Dischargeing Lerge quantities of Peutred matter being Painfull Offencive & Troublesome" (see Document 16). The selectmen of Rutland decided to care for Johnson because of his "helpless & Suffering Condition."[159] Johnson remained under the care of the town for nearly two years, and the selectmen asked the state for compensation in line with an earlier 1787 law about transient and idle people.[160] The Assembly granted Rutland the exorbitant sum of £73:19:9. This incident, along with another in Shoreham, encouraged the state to consider ways to revise the law and prevent idle and destitute people from receiving state funds. These events must be understood within the context of individual towns' responsibility for the care of poor inhabitants. The persistent problem of poor relief certainly influenced the lawmakers' concern about mounting costs associated with indigent people. However, the 1791 law did not simply focus on transient poor people, but went further by denying black people freedom and seeking to return fugitives to their owners. Although poverty and poor relief cut across race, age, and gender, the law seemed to single out African-descended people. Strikingly, the man who caused this law, John Johnson, had not been a slave, but rather a free man in the service of the French armed forces. Certain members of Vermont's Assembly attempted to use this example of indigence to repeal the law banning out-of-state sales of African Americans.

The 1791 Negro and Molatto Act deserves closer scrutiny. Its framers designed the law to place African Americans outside of the mainstream of civil society. As Elise Guyette notes, the proposal "was Vermont's first attempt at a fugitive slave law."[161] The authors introduced it because "Diverse Negroes, Molattoes, and persons held to Service in Other States & Kingdoms under the Laws of Such State or Kingdoms frequently Escape from their Masters or Owners and Run into this State and Doubts have arisen whither they are not thereby discharged from such Service or Labor."[162] They determined that the master or owner of any African American "held to Service or Labor" in any other state or country who had escaped to Vermont could retrieve their property. The law also threatened "any person or persons whatsoever [who] shall impede or hinder any such Master" in capturing an escaped slave with an £8 fine if convicted of helping a runaway. The law would have allowed slaveowners to use the "Civil power" to apprehend runaway slaves and be "removed to the State or Kingdom from whence he Escaped." The legislators also wanted to punish African Americans who "shall be found Strolling from Town to Town" as "Idle vagabond[s]" by warning them out of the state. If these people did not leave, the act would have allowed local authorities to indenture or bind them out to "hard Service" for up to three years. It offered two possible ways to avoid being bound out to hard labor. An individual freeholder could give £200 to the local justice of the peace as security that an African American would not become a government charge. Also, town meetings could vote a "Negro or Molattoe. . . . an inhabitant of that particular town," and if he or she became indigent the locality would have to accept financial responsibility.[163] The failed 1791 legislation made clear that some Vermonters did not take the abolition provision of the 1777 constitution as fixed policy.

The point of this law rested on the hope that Vermont would not become a haven for fugitive slaves, who some associated with disorder, chaos, and needless expense. The proposed Vermont law would have fined antislavery individuals for simply harboring or helping runaway slaves. At the same time, local authorities could be enlisted to help out-of-state slaveholders reclaim their runaways, though it remained unclear how much evidence they actually needed to present to a justice of the peace. These aspects of the law mirrored earlier legislation in other states. For example, Rhode Island's 1774 slave import law threatened to fine people who harbored runaway slaves, while Pennsylvania's 1780 Gradual Abolition Act also "established rights to recapture slaves, and to sue for damages anyone who harbored a slave."[164] The framers of the failed Vermont law wanted to control African Americans and make sure that fugitive slaves from New York or other states would not come to Vermont because of the fear that they would be returned to their owners or indentured under conditions that would have been akin to slavery.

Although the 1791 act did not become law, Vermont in practice refused to protect fugitive slaves within its borders. In this sense, Vermont followed the pattern established in other Northern states, where local governments "declined to protect fugitive slaves during abolition."[165] In the 1780s and 1790s, slaveholders advertised for their runaways in Vermont, offering rewards for the capture and return of the fugitives. The vast majority of advertisements in the *Vermont Gazette* appeared after the state had joined the Union (see Documents 18-20, 22-25).[166] Most runaways were male, spoke Dutch and English, and originated from New York. Some of them had spent part of their lives in Vermont. In 1786, one slaveholder complained about the loss of Mary Ann, a native of Africa with "several cuts on each side of her temple" (see Document 12).[167] In July 1791, Stephen Ball placed an advertisement in the *Vermont Gazette* to retain the services of his "negro man named BILL." Ball noted that Bill "calls himself a doctor, and has formerly followed that business in Shaftsbury and Arlington, in the state of Vermont" (see Document 18).[168] Clearly, slaveholders expected Vermonters to return runaways and local newspapers had no problem advertising for runaways despite the 1777 abolition of adult slavery. The newspapers had no interest in protecting fugitive slaves, and Vermonters were thought willing to return fugitives even before joining the Union. As the 1791 proposed legislation indicated, a minority of Vermonters viewed fugitive slaves and free black residents as unwanted social and economic burdens. Vermonters could oppose slavery in theory, but perhaps they also worried about the proliferation of an unwanted social subclass of fugitive slaves that would have increased the number of black people in the state.

Like its predecessors, the 1806 Act to Prevent Kidnapping specifically reveals the continuation of reenslavement and the problems that African Americans faced in Vermont (see Document 30). Legislators introduced this law because stealing and selling black people became so noticeable and embarrassing that the government felt pressured to initiate action. The law admitted that "there have been a number of instances of Negro persons, who were minors, having been transported by evil minded persons from this to the other States and [the] province of Canada, where slavery is established by law, and there disposed of as slaves."[169] Several issues arise from this blunt statement about the realities of slavery in the early nineteenth century. The sale and transportation of slaves to other states and Canada continued from 1777 to at least 1806, and government attempts to stop this nefarious traffic did not work. By 1806, Vermont's political leaders had realized that real enforcement was necessary to end slavery or prevent the sale of black people outside of the state. The Prevention of Kidnapping Act laid out harsh punishments, including a public whipping (up to 39 lashes), a fine, and imprisonment "not exceeding seven years." The criminal would also "be further liable to make good all damages" to the victim.[170] This bill finally gave teeth to the spirit of the 1777 abolition provision and the 1786 Sale and Transportation Act. The sale of an unknowable number of black people, especially young children, might have been prevented if the penalties adopted in 1806 had been adopted earlier to make the constitutional provision effective.

Despite the 1806 law, Vermont continued to allow "slave transit" and "slaveowner sojourns," which meant that masters could visit Vermont for extended time periods with their slaves without any pressure to free them.[171] Kevin Graffagnino shows that nineteenth-century Vermonters continued to hold various attitudes about slavery, and some fully supported the institution. Thus, it cannot be surprising that, as Marshall True points out, Burlington residents seem to have accepted slaveholding in their midst or remained blissfully and willfully ignorant of it.[172] In 1835, Ethan Allen's daughter Lucy Caroline Hitchcock migrated back to Burlington from Alabama along with two slaves (a mother and child). For at least six years, she owned slaves in Vermont before manumitting them after the female's husband had paid her a sum of money.[173] For six years, during the growing height of antislavery fervor in the 1830s, Hitchcock did not feel the need to free her slaves. Perhaps local people did not pressure her to do so. The Hitchcock episode demonstrates that slavery continued to persist in a free state—even one with deep commitments to antislavery ideology, especially by the late 1830s. For Hitchcock's two slaves, 35-year-old Lavinia and 12-year-old Francis, the contingent and inconsistent nature of Vermont attitudes toward slavery allowed the institution to persist.

REFLECTIONS ON THE MEANING AND ESSENCE
OF VERMONT SLAVERY

In early Vermont, freedom was not easily defined and various levels of unfreedom or bondage were imposed on black people, including child slavery, indentured servitude, and *de facto* slavery. The most basic understanding of legal slavery is that it attempts to make an individual human being into a piece of chattel property, but this basic and truthful definition has limitations. Even if the legality of slavery is eliminated, certain aspects of slavery can continue to exist. In his well-known study, sociologist Orlando Patterson's definition of slavery is based on the study of the institution across an array of societies and times. Patterson argues that slavery can be understood as "the permanent, violent domination of natally alienated and generally dishonored persons."[174] Slaves in Vermont fit this definition and even the 1777 abolition provision did not end the type of dishonoring that some free blacks suffered in the Green Mountain State. The most significant part of this definition of slavery is its emphasis on dishonor and the need of the master class to garner its own identity of superiority based on the alleged dishonor and inferiority of their slaves. As eminent historian David Brion Davis notes, there were "deep philosophic and psychological aspects to dishonoring, humiliating, or dehumanizing of slaves" that continued in the United States after emancipation in 1865, as illustrated by lynching and widespread racial hatred.[175] Davis makes the point that slaves were dehumanized because their "redeeming rational and spiritual qualities" were denied or diminished, and their alleged animalistic traits exaggerated and used to justify their enslavement and post-emancipation subordination.[176]

As these definitions indicate, some of the hallmarks of slavery, such as dishonoring, humiliation, and dehumanization are present in the documentation about the status and treatment of black people in early Vermont. After 1777, Vermont had forms of *de facto* slavery that violated the spirit of the constitutional abolition provision and the intent of the 1786 law prohibiting the sale and transportation of blacks out of the state. However informal or mediated, slavery in Vermont, while perhaps not dehumanizing black people in the same way as bondage in the sugar plantations of Barbados or the cotton plantations of the American South, still dishonored black people and exploited their labor. The legal end of adult slavery in Vermont still left African American children in a position where they could be "natally" alienated, and sometimes subjected to violence. The abolition provision of 1777 did not result in the establishment of meaningful freedom for many, perhaps the majority, of black people in Vermont. Instead, it allowed for the continued *de jure* exploitation of black children and the *de facto* persistence of slavery under the guise of terms such as "servant." The 1777 constitution marked a significant step in the direction of abolition, but it fell short of ending slavery in Vermont.

Taken together, what does the evidence considered in this study illuminate about slavery in Vermont? Historical documents including court cases, town histories, census records, legislative statutes, and other sources definitively establish the persistence of slavery between 1777 and 1806. The 1786 statute and the failed legislation of 1791 demonstrate that slavery and racial discrimination continued in certain parts of the state. In acknowledging Vermont's meaningful abolitionist past, historians must also come to grips with the continuation of slavery. The history of Afro-Vermonters must be treated with nuance, because their experience in the Green Mountain State included encounters with slavery and freedom, bondage and emancipation, and opportunities for citizenship alongside the obstacles of racism in the late eighteenth and early nineteenth centuries. Afro-Vermonters faced a broad spectrum of racial attitudes and various degrees of freedom and bondage. This study of slavery in Vermont is one small step, which follows the lead of earlier historians, in the process of reasserting the complexity of black history in the local context.

Notes

1. John A. Williams, ed., *State Papers of Vermont*, vol. 14: *Laws of Vermont* (Montpelier, Vt.: Secretary of State, 1966), 100.

2. E. P. Walton, ed., *Records of the Governor and Council of the State of Vermont*, 8 vols, (Montpelier, Vt.: Steam Press of J. & J. M. Poland, 1873-1880), 1: 92.

3. George W. Van Cleve, *A Slaveholders' Union: Slavery, Politics, and the Constitution in the Early American Republic* (Chicago: University of Chicago Press, 2010); Paul Finkelman, *Slavery and the Founders: Race and Liberty in the Age of Jefferson* (1996; second edition, Armonk: M. E. Sharpe, 2001); David Waldstreicher, *Slavery's Constitution: From Revolution to Ratification* (New York: Hill & Wang, 2009). On the issue of Northern emancipation and its problems and possibilities, see Paul Polgar, "'To Raise Them to an Equal Participation: Early National Abolitionism, Gradual Emancipation, and the Promise of African American Citizenship,'" *Journal of the Early* Republic 31 (Summer 2011): 229-58; Paul Polgar, "Standard Bearers of Liberty and Equality: Reinterpreting the Origins of American Abolitionism" (Ph.D. Dissertation, CUNY Graduate Center, 2013). Polgar persuasively argues that before the advent of the American Colonization Society, gradual emancipation or early American abolitionism hoped to halt white racism and make African Americans eventual citizens of the republic. This innovative interpretation presents a challenge to traditional accounts of gradual emancipation. In the case of Vermont, the end of slavery was not accompanied by a push to end racism or make black people citizens. Some Afro-Vermonters did achieve citizenship and a measure of equality, but many others did not achieve meaningful freedom in the Green Mountain State after the slow and torturous end of slavery. Other good books on this topic include: Van Cleve, *Slaveholders' Union*; David Gellman, *Emancipating New York: The Politics of Slavery and Freedom, 1777-1827* (Baton Rouge: Louisiana State University Press, 2006); Joanne P. Melish, *Disowning Slavery: "Race" and Gradual Emancipation in New England* (Ithaca, N.Y.: Cornell University Press, 1998); Gary B. Nash and Jean R. Soderlund, *Freedom by Degrees: Emancipation in Pennsylvania and Its Aftermath*

(New York: Oxford University Press, 1991); Shane White, *Somewhat More Independent: The End of Slavery in New York City, 1770-1810* (Athens: University of Georgia Press, 1991);Arthur Zilversmit, *The First Emancipation: The Abolition of Slavery in the North* (Chicago: University of Chicago Press, 1967); Leon F. Litwack, *North of Slavery: The Negro in the Free States, 1790-1860* (Chicago: University of Chicago Press, 1961).

4. Kari Winter greatly helped me to consider this important issue.

5. The 1791 act had different names, including: "An Act in addition to an Act intitled, An act providing for and ordering transient, idle, impotent and poor persons,"; see "Act Respecting Negr[oes] & Molattoes," January 24, 1791, Volume 3, page 80, Manuscript Vermont State Papers, 1777-1861, (series SE-118). SE118-00003. Vermont State Archives and Records Administration, Middlesex; and "An act to enable the masters of slaves or servants who escape from them, to apprehend such slaves or servants, and carry them out of this state and to enable the selectmen of the several towns of this state to bind out to service such free negroes as appear to them indolent, vicious, or likely to become chargeable to the public," in Walter H. Crockett, ed., *State Papers of Vermont*, vol. 3, part 4: *Journals and Proceedings of the State of Vermont* (Bellows Falls: The Wyndham Press, 1929), 225; Bennington Friendly Society, Minute Book, April 10, 1789, 57, Special Collections, Bailey/Howe Library, University of Vermont, Burlington.

6. Barre-Montpelier *Times-Argus*, February 1, 2009, citing an uncatalogued pamphlet, "Negroes in Vermont," Vermont Historical Society, Barre. Raymond P. Zirblis's talk, "A Grain of Salt: Slavery in Vermont's Colonial and Early Statehood Eras," can be found at the Center for Research on Vermont, University of Vermont, Burlington, and online at: http://www.retn.org/programs/grain-salt-slavery-vermonts-colonial-and-early-statehood-eras.

7. Raymond P. Zirblis, "Slavery in Vermont," in John J. Duffy, Samuel B. Hand, and Ralph H. Orton, eds., *The Vermont Encyclopedia* (Hanover, N.H.: University Press of New England, 2003), 271.

8. Gretchen H. Gerzina, *Mr. and Mrs. Prince: How an Extraordinary Eighteenth-Century Family Moved Out of Slavery and into Legend* (New York: Amistad, 2008), 145-88.

9. On the opportunities and obstacles facing black people in early Vermont, see Kari J. Winter, "The Strange Career of Benjamin Franklin Prentiss, Antislavery Lawyer," *Vermont History* 79 (Summer/Fall 2011): 121-40; Kari J. Winter, "Bordering Freedom but Unable to Cross into the Promised Land: Africans in Early Vermont," *Historical Reflections* 32 (2006): 473-92; Elise A. Guyette, *Discovering Black Vermont: African American Farmers in Hinesburgh, 1790-1870* (Lebanon, N.H.: University of Vermont Press, published by the University Press of New England, 2010); Gerzina, *Mr. and Mrs. Prince*; Kari J. Winter, *The Blind African Slave: Or the Memoirs of Boyrereau Brinch Nicknamed Jeffrey Brace* (Madison: University of Wisconsin Press, 2005); John Saillant, *Black Puritan, Black Republican: The Life and Thought of Lemuel Haynes, 1753-1833* (Oxford: Oxford University Press, 2003); Jane Williamson, "Row-

land T. Robinson, Rokeby, and the Underground Railroad in Vermont," *Vermont History* 69 (Winter 2001): 19-31. John M. Lovejoy, "Racism in Antebellum Vermont," *Vermont History* 69 (Winter 2001): 48-65.

10. Abby M. Hemenway, ed., *The Vermont Historical Gazetteer*, 5 vols. (vol. 1: Burlington, Vt.: Miss A. M. Hemenway, 1867; vol. 2: Burlington, Vt.: Miss A. M. Hemenway, 1871; vol. 3: Claremont, N.H.: The Claremont Manufacturing Company, 1877; vol. 4: Montpelier, Vt.: Vermont Watchman and State Journal Press, 1882; vol. 5: Brandon, Vt.: Mrs. Carrie E. H. Page, 1891), 1: 163; Walton, *Records of the Governor and Council*, 1: 93.

11. "Prof Says Vermont's Antislavery Reputation Is Not the Whole Truth," *Seven Days*, February 4, 2009, accessed September 7, 2012, http://www.7dvt.com/2009prof-says-vermonts-antislavery-reputation-not-whole-truth. On the problem of freedom and opportunities for escape in the nineteenth century, see Raymond P. Zirblis, *Friends of Freedom: The Vermont Underground Railroad Survey Report* (Montpelier, Vt.: Division for Historic Preservation, 1996).

12. John W. Sweet, *Bodies Politic: Negotiating Race in the American North, 1730-1830* (Baltimore: Johns Hopkins University Press, 2003).

13. Saillant, *Black Puritan*, 71-72.

14. Ibid., 62.

15. On the expansion of slavery and racism, see Adam Rothman, *Slave Country: American Expansion and the Origins of the Deep South* (Cambridge, Mass.: Harvard University Press, 2005). The colonization movement sought to relocate black people to Africa.

16. Elise A. Guyette, "Black Lives and White Racism in Vermont,1760-1870" (Master's Thesis, University of Vermont, 1992), 148, 152.

17. Ira Berlin, *Many Thousands Gone: The First Two Centuries of Slavery in North America* (Cambridge, Mass.: Harvard University Press, 1998), 229.

18. Peter Kolchin, *American Slavery, 1619-1877* (1993; second edition, New York: Hill & Wang, 2003), 78.

19. David Brion Davis, *Inhuman Bondage: The Rise and Fall of Slavery in the New World* (New York: Oxford University Press, 2006), 152.

20. David Brion Davis, *The Problem of Slavery in the Age of Revolution, 1770-1823* (1975; reprint, New York: Oxford University Press, 1999), 78.

21. Winthrop Jordan, *White Over Black: American Attitudes Toward the Negro, 1550-1812* (Chapel Hill: University of North Carolina Press, 1968), 345.

22. Edgar J. McManus, *Black Bondage in the North* (Syracuse, N.Y.: Syracuse University Press, 1973), 160.

23. Finkelman, *Slavery and the Founders*, 57.

24. Waldstreicher, *Slavery's Constitution*, 49, 60.

25. John P. Kaminski, ed., *A Necessary Evil? Slavery and the Debate Over the Constitution* (Madison, Wisc.: Madison House, 1995), 9.

26. Van Cleve, *Slaveholders' Union*, 57.

27. Anne Farrow, Joel Lang, and Jennifer Frank, *Complicity: How the North Pro-

moted, Prolonged, and Profited From Slavery (New York: Ballantine, 2006), xiv.

28. Antonio T. Bly, ed., *Escaping Bondage: A Documentary History of Runaway Slaves in Eighteenth-Century New England, 1700-1789* (Lanham, Md.: Lexington Books, 2012).

29. Gordon S. Wood, *Empire of Liberty: A History of the Early Republic, 1789-1815* (New York: Oxford University Press, 2009), 519.

30. Norman K. Risjord, *Jefferson's America, 1760-1815* (Lanham, Md.: Rowman & Littlefield, 2010), 184.

31. Francis D. Cogliano, *Revolutionary America: A Political History, 1763-1815* (London: Routledge, 2000), 187.

32. Francis Jennings, *The Creation of America: Through Revolution to Empire* (New York: Cambridge University Press, 2000), 287.

33. Bernard Bailyn, *The Ideological Origins of the American Revolution* (1967; second edition, Cambridge, Mass.: Harvard University Press, 1992), 246.

34. Gordon S. Wood, *The Radicalism of the American Revolution* (New York: Alfred A. Knopf, 1992), 186-87.

35. Waldstreicher, *Slavery's Constitution*, 12; see also 10-11, 162.

36. Daniel Chipman, *A Memoir of Thomas Chittenden, the First Governor of Vermont; with a history of the constitution during his administration* (Middlebury, Vt.: Published by the Author, 1849), 82-83.

37. Zilversmit, *The First Emancipation*, 116.

38. Saillant, *Black Puritan*.

39. Melish, *Disowning Slavery*, 64.

40. T. D. Seymour Bassett, *The Gods of the Hills: Piety and Society in Nineteenth-Century Vermont* (Montpelier: Vermont Historical Society, 2000), 36. Bassett wrote "Westminster" but meant to say "Windsor."

41. Winter, *The Blind African Slave.*

42. Zirblis, "A Grain of Salt"; Elise A. Guyette, "The Working Lives of African Vermonters in Census and Literature," *Vermont History* 61 (Spring 1993): 69-84; Guyette, "Black Lives in White Vermont," 13; Guyette, *Discovering Black Vermont*; J. Kevin Graffagnino, "Vermont Attitudes Toward Slavery: The Need For A Closer Look," *Vermont History* 61 (Winter 1977): 31-34; Marshall M. True, "Slavery in Burlington? An Historical Note," *Vermont History* 50 (Fall 1982): 227-230.

43. Bailyn, *Ideological Origins of the American Revolution*, 233.

44. Ibid., 235.

45. F. Nwabueze Okoye, "Chattel Slavery as the Nightmare of the American Revolutionaries," *William and Mary Quarterly*, Third Series, 37 (1980): 3-28; see also Patricia Bradley, *Slavery, Propaganda, and the American Revolution* (Jackson: University Press of Mississippi, 1998).

46. François Furstenberg, "Beyond Freedom and Slavery: Autonomy, Virtue, and Resistance in Early American Political Discourse," *Journal of American History* 89 (March 2003): 1295-1330.

47. Jack P. Greene, "'Slavery or Independence': Some Reflections on the

Relationship Among Liberty, Black Bondage, and Equality in Revolutionary South Carolina," *South Carolina Historical Magazine* 80 (July 1979): 193-214.

48. Peter A. Dorsey, *Common Bondage: Slavery as Metaphor in Revolutionary America* (Knoxville: University of Tennessee Press, 2009), xviii.

49. Ethan Allen, *A Vindication of the Opposition of the Inhabitants of Vermont to the Government of New-York and of their right to form into an independent state: humbly submitted to the consideration of the impartial world* (Dresden: Alden Spooner, 1779), 42.

50. Michael Sherman, Gene Sessions, and P. Jeffrey Potash, *Freedom and Unity: A History of Vermont* (Barre: Vermont Historical Society, 2004), 84.

51. John J. Duffy, et al., eds., *Ethan Allen and His Kin: Correspondence, 1772-1819*, 2 vols. (Hanover, N.H.: University Press of New England, 1998), 1: 34.

52. Allen, *Vindication*, 7.

53. Ibid., 61-62.

54. Randolph A. Roth, *The Democratic Dilemma: Religion, Reform, and Social Order in the Connecticut River Valley of Vermont, 1791-1850* (Cambridge: Cambridge University Press, 1987), 23-24.

55. Furstenberg, "Beyond Freedom and Slavery," 1295-1330.

56. Duffy, *Ethan Allen and his Kin*, 1: 184.

57. J. Kevin Graffagnino, "Revolution and Empire on the Northern Frontier: Ira Allen of Vermont, 1751-1814," (Ph.D. diss., University of Massachusetts, 1993), 12.

58. Duffy, *Ethan Allen and his Kin*, 1: 166; for a note on his slave, see 165.

59. *Vermont Gazette*, August 28, 1783.

60. "Prof. Says Vermont's Antislavery Reputation is Not the Whole Truth"; Zirblis, "Slavery in Vermont," 270-71.

61. There have been several excellent studies about slavery in the North, including but not limited to the following works: Allegra di Bonaventura, *For Adam's Sake: A Family Saga in Colonial New England* (New York: W. W. Norton, 2013); C. S. Manegold, *Ten Hills Farm: The Forgotten History of Slavery in the North* (Princeton, N.J.: Princeton University Press, 2010); Farrow, Lang, and Frank, *Complicity*; William D. Piersen, *Black Yankees: The Development of an Afro-American Subculture in Eighteenth-Century New England* (Amherst: University of Massachusetts Press, 1988); McManus, *Black Bondage in the North*; Lorenzo J. Greene, *The Negro in Colonial New England* (1942; reprint, New York: Atheneum, 1968), 98; Melish, *Disowning Slavery*, 1-46; Berlin, *Many Thousands Gone*, 177-94; Robert K. Fitts, *Inventing New England's Slave Paradise: Master/Slave Relations in Eighteenth-Century Narragansett, Rhode Island* (New York: Garland, 1998); Robert E. Desrochers, "Slave-For-Sale Advertisements and Slavery in Massachusetts, 1704-1781," *William and Mary Quarterly* 59 (July 2002): 623-64; Sarah Deutsch, "The Elusive Guineamen: Newport Slavers, 1735-1774," *New England Quarterly* 55 (1982): 229-53; Rachel C. Lin, "The Rhode Island Slave-Traders: Butchers, Bakers, and Candlestick-Makers," *Slavery and Abolition* 23 (December 2002): 21-38; Graham R. Hodges, *Slavery and Freedom in the Rural North: African Americans in Monmouth County, New Jersey, 1665-1865* (Madison, Wisc.: Madison House, 1997); Leslie M. Harris, *In the Shadow of Slavery: African*

Americans in New York City, 1626-1863 (Chicago: University of Chicago Press, 2003);
Eric J. Roth, "'The Society of Negroes Unsettled': A History of Slavery in New Paltz,
N.Y.," *Afro-Americans in New York Life and History* 27 (2003): 27-54; Ira Berlin and
Leslie M. Harris, eds., *Slavery in New York* (New York: The New Press, 2005); see
Duncan Faherty's review of Berlin and Harris and the exhibit about slavery in New
York, "'It Happened Here': Slavery on the Hudson," *American Quarterly* 58 (2006):
455-66; Gellman, *Emancipating New York*; White, *Somewhat More Independent*;
Thelma W. Foote, *Black and White Manhattan: The History of Racial Formation in
Colonial New York City* (New York: Oxford University Press, 2004); Richard S. Moss,
*Slavery on Long Island: A Study in Local Institutional and Early African American Com-
munal Life* (New York: Garland, 1993); Peter Benes, ed., *Slavery/Antislavery in New
England—The Dublin Seminar for New England Folklife Annual Proceedings, 2003* (Bos-
ton: Boston University, 2005); Sweet, *Bodies Politic*; Shane White, "Slavery in the
North," *Magazine of History* 17 (2003): 17-21; Jill Lepore, *New York Burning: Liberty,
Slavery, and Conspiracy in Eighteenth-Century Manhattan* (New York: Knopf, 2005);
see also Brendan McConville's critical review, "Of Slavery and Sources," *Reviews
in American History* 34 (2006): 281-90; James Oliver Horton and Lois E. Horton,
*In Hope of Liberty: Culture, Community and Protest Among Northern Free Blacks,
1700-1860* (New York: Oxford University Press, 1997); John Saillant, ed., "'Some
Thoughts on the Subject of Freeing the Negro Slaves in the Colony of Connecticut,
Humbly Offered to the Consideration of All Friends to Liberty & Justice," by Levi
Hart," *New England Quarterly* 75 (March 2002): 107-28. Graham Russell Hodges,
Root and Branch: African Americans in New York and East Jersey, 1613-1863 (Chapel
Hill: University of North Carolina, 1999).

62. *Historical Statistics of the United States, Colonial Times to 1970*, 2 vols. (Washington, D.C.: Bureau of the Census, 1975, Bicentennial edition), 2: 1168, 1171.

63. Zirblis, "Slavery in Vermont," 270.

64. Ibid.

65. Zirblis, "A Grain of Salt"; "Negroes in Vermont," cited in *Times-Argus*, February 1, 2009.

66. P. J. Staudenraus, *The African Colonization Movement, 1816-1865* (New York:
Columbia University Press, 1961); Eric Burin, *Slavery and the Peculiar Solution: A
History of the American Colonization Society* (Gainesville: University Press of Florida,
2005); Matthew Hannon, "From Vermont to Liberia: An Examination of the Vermont Colonization Society," (Master's Thesis, University of Vermont, 2008).

67. Melish, *Disowning Slavery*, 64-79; Zilversmit; *The First Emancipation*, 98-214;
Van Cleve, *Slaveholders' Union*, 59-100.

68. Gary J. Aichele, "Making the Vermont Constitution: 1777-1824," *Vermont
History* 57 (Summer 1988): 180; Peter S. Onuf, "State-Making in Revolutionary
America: Independent Vermont as a Case Study," *Journal of American History* 67
(March 1981): 797-815; the best discussion might be Graffagnino, "Revolution and
Empire on the Northern Frontier," 73-157.

69. Walton, *Records of the Governor and Council*, 1: 92.

70. Roth, *Democratic Dilemma*, 23.

71. Alistair W. W. MacCabe, "The Story of the No-Slavery Clause of the Republic of Vermont, 1777" (Unpublished undergraduate paper, Eisenhower College, 1971), Vermont State Archives and Records Administration, Middlesex.

72. Kaminski, *A Necessary Evil*, 14.

73. *State Papers of Vermont*, vol. 3, part 1: *Journals and Proceedings of the General Assembly of the State of Vermont* (Bellows Falls: P. H. Gobie Press, 1924), 48.

74. *The Constitution of the State of Vermont, As Revised by the Council of Censors and Recommended for the Consideration of the People* (Windsor, Vt.: Hough and Spooner, 1785).

75. Jordan, *White Over Black*, 351.

76. For example, David Menschel, "Abolition without Deliverance: The Law of Connecticut Slavery, 1784-1848," *Yale Law Review* 111 (2001): 183-222.

77. Kaminski, *A Necessary Evil*, 14.

78. Ibid., 29.

79. Van Cleve, *Slaveholders' Union*, 74.

80. Guyette, *Discovering Black Vermont*, 6-7; Guyette, "Black Lives," 67-98; Winter, *Blind African Slave*, 58-59.

81. Robert Mello, *Moses Robinson and the Founding of Vermont* (Barre: Vermont Historical Society, forthcoming), chapter 10.

82. Isaac Jennings, *Memorials of a Century* (Boston: Gould and Lincoln, 1869), 63.

83. Ibid., 62-64.

84. David Avery, *A Narrative of the Rise and Progress of the Difficulties which have issued in Separation between the Minister and People of Bennington, 1783* (Bennington, Vt.: Haswell and Russell, 1783).

85. Mello, *Moses Robinson*, chapter 10.

86. Mary G. Nye, ed. *State Papers of Vermont*, Volume 6: *Sequestration, Confiscation, Sale of Estates* (Montpelier, Vt.: Secretary of State, 1941), 253.

87. Mello, *Moses Robinson*, chapter 8; Benjamin H. Hall, *History of Eastern Vermont: From its Earliest Settlement to the Close of the Eighteenth Century* (New York: D. Appleton & Co., 1858), 331.

88. *Pompee Brakkee Versus Elijah Lovel*, June 10, 1779, Supreme Court 1779, vol. 1, p. 10, Vermont Superior Court, Rutland Unit, Rutland.

89. John Armstrong, 1782 Probate Record, Vermont Superior Court, Bennington Probate Division, Bennington.

90. Samuel Andrew, Bill of Sale, April 1783, Special Collections, Bailey/Howe Library, University of Vermont. There is another bill of sale from 1770 attached to this document: John Barrett purchased a nine year old named Rose from Caleb Bull. Barrett's name is also spelled "Barratt" in some documents. Topsham John Barrett Papers, Topsham, Vermont.

91. Guyette, "Black Lives," 13.

92. Charles H. Hubbard and Justus Dartt, *History of the Town of Springfield,*

Vermont (Boston: George H. Walker & Co., 1895), 489. The record remains mute about Anthony's parents and how long he had been separated from them. However, it is possible that Dinah might have been Anthony's mother as she lived in Jotham White's house around the time the boy was born.

93. Cited in Melish, *Disowning Slavery*, 66.

94. Hubbard and Dartt, *History of the Town of Springfield*, 489; Marcel Trudel, *Dictionnaire des esclaves et de leurs proprietaries au Canada français* (Ville LaSalle: Hurtubise Cahiers du Québec, 1990), 14.

95. Jotham White, typed copy of Bill of Sale of a Negro Woman Slave, Dinah, executed to Stephen Jacob, July 26, 1783, XMS 326 W582, Vermont Historical Society.

96. Ibid.

97. Jennifer Morgan, *Laboring Women: Reproduction and Gender in New World Slavery* (Philadelphia: University of Pennsylvania Press, 2004); *Journal of Women's History* (June 2007), issue about slave women.

98. *Heads of Families at the First Census of the United States Taken in the Year 1790, Vermont* (Washington, D.C.: Government Printing Office, 1907), 66; *Heads of Families at the Second Census of the United States Taken in the Year 1800, Vermont* (Montpelier: Vermont Historical Society, 1938), 180.

99. Royall Tyler, ed., *Reports of Cases Argued and Determined in the Supreme Court of Judicature of the State of Vermont*, 2 vols. (New York: I. Riley, 1809-1810), 2: 197.

100. Katherine E. Conlin, "Dinah and the Slave Question in Vermont," *Vermont Quarterly* 21 (October 1953): 289-91.

101. H. S. Wardner, "Judge Jacob and his Dinah," *The Vermonter: The State Magazine* (May-June, 1914): 80-88; Conlin, "Dinah and the Slave Question," 289-91; Honorable John H. Watson, "In Re Vermont Constitution of 1777, as Regards its Adoption, and its Declaration Forbidding Slavery; and the Subsequent Existence of Slavery Within the Territory of the Sovereign State," an address delivered to the Vermont Bar Association, January 4, 1921; Mark Bushnell, *It Happened in Vermont* (Guilford, Ct.: Globe Pequot Press, 2009), 29-32; Tyler, *Reports of Cases*, 2: 192-201. See also Aviam Soifer, "De Facto Slavery and the 'Syren Songs of Liberty and Equality': Carol Weisbrod, Much Obliged," *Connecticut Law Review* 40 (July 2008): 1317-1328.

102. Wardner, "Judge Jacob," 81.

103. Ibid., 81-82

104. Tyler, Reports of Cases, 2: 193.

105. Ibid.

106. Ibid.

107. Ibid., 2: 194.

108. Ibid., 2: 196.

109. Ibid., 2: 197.

110. Ibid., 2: 197-98. By "warning out," officials demanded a person leave town.

111. Ibid., 2: 201.

112. *Spooner's Vermont Journal* reported the death of both Jacob and Dinah, but did not mention his slaveholding; see March 6, 1809, February 3, 1817.

113. Tyler, *Reports of Cases*, 2: 192, 199.

114. Duffy, *Ethan Allen and his Kin*, 1: 165; and http://cdi.uvm.edu/findingaids/collection/allenfamily.ead.xml, accessed October 1, 2012. Levi Allen's Prince might have been Prince Robinson, who later worked for Samuel Harrington. Prince Robinson was married and received a war pension. Thanks to Gary Shattuck for this information.

115. My knowledge of Ethan Allen's black slaves comes from the work of John Duffy and I am thankful to him for sharing his research with me. John Duffy to Harvey Amani Whitfield, November 11, 2012. It is also likely, according to Duffy, that Ethan Allen owned slaves in the 1760s in Northampton, Massachusetts; also see Guyette, "Black Lives," 15.

116. Keith R. Barney, *The History of Springfield, Vermont, 1885-1961, With an Introductory Chapter to 1885* (Springfield, Vt.: William L. Bryant Foundation, 1972), 24; "Negroes in Vermont," cited in *Times-Argus*, February 1, 2009.

117. Allen P. Beach, *The Basin Harbor Story* (Vergennes, Vt.: Basin Harbor Club, 1963), 5-6.

118. Hemenway, *Vermont Historical Gazetteer*, 2: 370.

119. Greene, *The Negro in Colonial New England*, 98.

120. Hemenway, *Vermont Historical Gazetteer*, 2: 372.

121. Almira D. Stewart, "Memoirs," Vermont Manuscript Files, Special Collections, Bailey/Howe Library, University of Vermont.

122. Population Schedules, 3rd Census, 1810, Vermont, NARA #M252, Reel 65, #2, Special Collections, Bailey/Howe Library, University of Vermont, Burlington.

123. Harvey Amani Whitfield, "The Struggle Over Slavery in the Maritime Colonies," *Acadiensis* 41 (Summer/Autumn 2012): 17-44; on various types of bondage, see John Donoghue, "'Out of the Land of Bondage': The English Revolution and the Atlantic Origins of Abolition," *American Historical Review* 115 (October 2010): 943-74.

124. *Heads of Families, 1790*, 8.

125. Walton, *Records of the Governor and Council*, 4: 425.

126. *Heads of Families, 1790*, 8. For a different opinion of the 1791 census, see Betty Bandel, "'Satisfaction Brought It Back'" *Vermont History News* 30 (Nov.-Dec. 1979), 91-92.

127. Winter, "Africans in Early Vermont," 477.

128. *Heads of Families, 1790*, 16

129. Ibid., 10.

130. Ibid., 47, 48, 52, 12.

131. *Heads of Families, 1800*, 15, 137, 154. Saxton's last name is spelled "Sexton" in this source and it seems that Henry Cole moved to Guilford and Nathaniel Foster to Wilmington.

132. *Heads of Families, 1790*, 66; *Heads of Families, 1800*, 180.

133. *Heads of Families, 1790*, 64.

134. Mary E. Baker, *Folklore of Springfield* (Springfield, Vt.: NP, 1922), 63.

135. *Heads of Families, 1800*, 29.

136. Zirblis, "A Grain of Salt"; "Negroes in Vermont," cited in *Times-Argus*, February 1, 2009.

137. Williams, *Laws of Vermont*, 100.

138. Van Cleve, *Slaveholders' Union*, 81.

139. Ibid., 82; Nash and Soderland, *Freedom by Degrees*.

140. Melish, *Disowning Slavery*, 74; Van Cleve, *Slaveholders' Union*, 88-89.

141. Van Cleve, *Slaveholders' Union*, 90.

142. Walton, *Records of the Governor and Council*, 3: 473.

143. Windsor (Vermont) *Morning Ray*, July 10, 1792.

144. Kaminski, *A Necessary Evil*, 112.

145. *Journals of the General Assembly of the State of Vermont* [1805] (Windsor, Vt.: Alden Spooner, 1806), 14.

146. Ibid., 54.

147. For the act to repeal the 1786 Transportation and Sale Act, see Crockett, *State Papers of Vermont*, vol. 3, part 4, 225; "An Act Respecting Negr[oes] & Molattoes."

148. Melish, *Disowning Slavery*, 163-237.

149. Walton, *Records of the Governor and Council*, 5: 412.

150. Ibid., 5: 413.

151. *Journals of the General Assembly of the State of Vermont* [1804] (Bennington, Vt.: Haswell & Smead, 1805), 267.

152. The 1791 act had different names, see note 5 above.

153. Tyler, *Reports of Cases*, 2: 200.

154. Crockett, *Journals and Proceedings*, vol. 4, part 3, 225.

155. Ibid., 244.

156. Ibid., 178-80, 269.

157. Ibid., 269.

158. Carolyn Stone, "A Monograph on an Act Introduced in the Vermont General Assembly on 24 January 1791 Respecting Negr[oes] & Molattoes," unpublished paper, Vermont State Archives and Records Administration, Middlesex.

159. Edward A. Hoyt, ed., *State Papers of Vermont*, vol. 9: *General Petitions, 1788-1792* (Montpelier, Vt.: Howard E. Armstrong, Secretary of State, 1955), 281.

160. Ibid., 281-82.

161. Guyette, *Discovering Black Vermont*, 33.

162. "Act Respecting Negr[oes] & Molattoes."

163. Ibid.

164. Van Cleve, *Slaveholders' Union*, 91.

165. Ibid.; Finkelman, *Slavery and the Founders*, 98-104.

166. Runaway slave advertisements can be found in the following editions of the *Vermont Gazette*: July 27, 1792; October 19, 1792; March 22, 1793; April 19, 1793;

June 28, 1793; August 14, 1795.

167. *Vermont Gazette*, July 3, 1786.

168. Ibid., July 25, 1791.

169. Walton, *Records of the Governor and Council*, 5: 131.

170. *Acts and Laws Passed by the Legislature of the State of Vermont* (Bennington, Vt.: Anthony Haswell, 1806), 152.

171. Van Cleve, *Slaveholders' Union*, 61.

172. Graffagnino, "Vermont Attitudes Toward Slavery," 31-34; True, "Slavery in Burlington," 227-230.

173. True, "Slavery in Burlington," 228-29.

174. Orlando Patterson, *Slavery and Social Death: A Comparative Study* (Cambridge, Mass.: Harvard University Press, 1982), 13.

175. Davis, *Inhuman Bondage*, 31.

176. Ibid., 32.

Primary Source Documents

Wallingford July 5th 1770

John Barrett Bought

of Caleb Bull

A Negro Garl About Nine years of Age, Named Rose, which I Delever to Said Barrett Sound and well as My Own Proper Estate, for the Consideration of Thirty four Pounds Lawfull Money Paid to Me

Caleb Bull

Wit:

Joseph Robinson

Eunice Robinson

Huldah Robinson

BILL OF SALE, JOHN BARRETT PURCHASED ROSE (1770)

Overview: John Barrett purchased Rose from Caleb Bull in Wallingford, Connecticut, and probably brought her to the New Hampshire Grants in 1771 or 1772. (See Frederick W. Richardson, *Eighteenth-Century Springfield: From Wilderness to Vermont Statehood, 1751-1791* [Springfield, self-published, 1991], 206.) The document offers no information about Rose's biological parents or her background. We know very little about this young slave—her place of birth; where her parents resided; what type of work she did; and how Caleb Bull became her owner. Sadly, significant parts of the lives of black girls like Rose have been lost to Vermont historians.

Source: Bill of Sale, John Barrett purchased Rose from Caleb Bull, 1770, attached to Samuel Andrew, Bill of Sale, April 1783. Topsham John Barrett Papers, Town of Topsham, Vermont, at Special Collections, Bailey/Howe Library, University of Vermont, Burlington.

Wallingford, July 5th, 1770

John Barrett Bought of Caleb Bull a Negro garl about nine years of age named Rose which of Deliver to said Barrett Sound and Well as My Own Proper Estate, for the consideration of Thirty Five Pounds Lawfull Money Recd of me

Caleb Bull

knows to what degree of earthly happiness Mankind may attain by perfecting the arts of government; in permitting the People of this State, by common Consent, and without violence, deliberately to form for themselves such just rules as they shall think best for governing their future Society; And being fully convinced that it is our indispensable duty, to establish such original Principles of Government as will best promote the General Happiness of the People of this State, and their Posterity, and provide for future Improvements, without Partiality for, or Prejudice against, any particular Class, Sect, or Denomination of Men whatever; Do, by virtue of Authority vested in us, by our Constituents, ordain, declare and establish the following declaration of Rights, and Frame of Government, to be the Constitution of this Commonwealth, and to remain in force therein forever, unaltered, except in such Articles, as shall hereafter on Experience be found to require improvement, and which shall, by the same Authority of the People, fairly delegated, as this frame of Government directs, be amended or improved, for the more effectual obtaining and securing the great End and design of all government, herein before mentioned.

Chapter 1

A Declaration of the Rights of the Inhabitants of the State of Vermont.

1. That all men are born equally free and independent, and have certain natural, inherent and unalianable Rights, amongst which are the enjoying and defending Life and Liberty; acquiring, possessing and protecting Property, and pursuing and obtaining Happiness and Safety. — Therefore, no male person, born in this Country, or brought from over Sea, ought to be holden by Law to serve any person as a Servant, Slave or Apprentice, after he arrives to the age of twenty one Years, nor female in like manner, after she arrives to the age of eighteen Years, unless they are bound by their own Consent after they arrive to such Age, or bound by Law for the Payment of Debts, Damages, Fines, Costs, or the like.

2. That private Property ought to be subservient to public Uses when necessity requires it; nevertheless, whenever any particular man's Property is taken for the Use of the public, the Owner ought to receive an equivalent in Money.

Abolition of Adult Slavery (1777)

Overview: The Vermont provision that banned adult slavery is one of the earliest examples of abolition in the New World. Its significance as one of the first instances of slavery's abolition in the British Empire cannot be overstated. However, if read carefully, the Vermont Constitution left certain loopholes that allowed child slavery, and in the years immediately following, legislators failed to add enforcement mechanisms to ensure the end of slavery, until 1786.

Source: Vermont Constitution, Chapter 1, "A Declaration of the Rights of the Inhabitants of the State of Vermont," Vermont Constitution 1777 (A-014). MAP-A28.4. Vermont State Archives and Records Administration, Middlesex. See also E. P. Walton, ed., *Records of the Governor and Council of the State of Vermont*, 8 vols. (Montpelier, Vt.: Steam Press of J & J. M. Poland, 1873-1880), 1: 92.

I. That all men are born equally free and independent, and have certain natural, inherent and unalianable Rights, amongst which are the enjoying and defending Life and Liberty; acquiring, possessing and protecting Property, and pursuing and obtaining Happiness and Safety. Therefore, no male person, born in this country, or brought from over sea, ought to be holden by Law to serve any person as a Servant, Slave or Apprentice, after he arrives to the age of twenty-one years, nor female in like manner, after she arrives to the age of eighteen years, unless they are bound by their own consent after they arrive at such age, or bound by Law for the Payment of Debts, Damages, Fines, Costs, or the like.

dence in that place he removed to Tinmouth, which had then reached an advanced stage of settlement.

In 1775 Col. Allen was appointed captain of a company of minute men, which was afterwards made a part of Col. Samuel Herrick's famous Regiment of Rangers, and participated with them in many sanguinary encounters and perilous adventures. On the 10th of May, 1775 Capt. Allen formed one of the party under Gen. Ethan Allen in the memorable capture of Ticonderoga. He was one of the delegates from Tinmouth to the general convention held at Cephas Kent's house in Dorset, Sept. 25, 1776, on which occasion certain resolutions were adopted substantially declaring the New Hampshire Grants "a free and separate district," and renouncing the authority of the New York government. He was also chosen one of the delegates from Tinmouth to the convention held at Windsor in July, 1777, that formed our first State constitution. After the dissolution of the convention he moved his family to Bennington. Aug. 16, 1777, was fought the decisive battle at that place, in which Capt. Allen bore a conspicuous part,—signalizing himself by great bravery and efficiency both as a soldier and commanding officer. At one time during the engagement, he with only 30 men, under the cover of a natural breastwork of rocks, successfully contended against the main body of Col. Baum's troops of Burgoyne's army, causing great slaughter among them, and a temporary retreat.

In the early part of September, 1777, Gen. Lincoln, then in command of the frontier department, despatched 1500 men from Pawlet, in three divisions, to follow in the rear of Burgoyne's army. These divisions were commanded respectively by Colonels Johnson, Woodbury, and Brown. The forces of Cols. Johnson and Woodbury were sent to attack Mt. Independence (Orwell), and Skeenesborough (now Whitehall). Capt. Allen's company were attached to Col. Brown's division. Col. Brown's forces were designed to attack Ticonderoga, Mount Defiance, Mount Hope, and one or two other strategic points of lesser importance, and to liberate 100 American prisoners in the hands of the British at Ticonderoga, and if possible, to effect the capture of the British flotilla at that place. Col. Brown assigned to Capt. Allen the taking of Mt. Defiance, opposite Ticonderoga, which was considered an almost impregnable fortress, and was at this time defended by about 200 British regulars, with artillery. He accomplished this hazardous undertaking, with the assistance of Lieut. Isaac Clark and 40 Green Mountain rifle rangers early on the morning of Sept. 18, 1777, by surprise, and without the loss of a single man. After performing this brilliant achievement, he rejoined Col. Brown's division, which, with those of Cols. Johnson and Woodbury, a few days later joined Gen. Gates's army investing Burgoyne's forces, and were in the action at Saratoga, Oct. 7, 1777. After the enemy's capitulation, Capt. Allen joined his family at Bennington, but subsequently returned with them to Tinmouth. During the latter part of this year he was for a time in command of a small detachment of State troops at Pawlet.*

The record of Col. Allen's military service is far from complete. Aside from the details of his career already given, it is positively known that he was commander of the fort at Vergennes either in 1778, or the following year; and that he performed important and effective military service during the war, mainly on the western side of Lake Champlain. While he resided on the Island he would relate to his guests (pointing towards Essex Landing, N. Y.), "With about the same number of *Green Mountain Boys*, I captured

* The following document issued by Col. Allen, while in command at Pawlet, is from the records of Bennington, *verbatim*, and serves to show what some of our ancestors thought of Slavery.

"Head Quarters Pollet }
28th of November 1777.}

To whom it may Concern Know ye Whereas Dinah Mattis, a negro woman with nancey her Child of two months old was taken Prisnor on Lake Champlain, with the British Troops Some where near Col Gilliner's Patten the Twelth day of Instant November by a Scout under my Command, and according to a Resolve Past by the Honnorable Continental Congress that all Prisses belong to the Captivators thereof—therefore She and her Child became the just Property of the Captivators thereof—I being Conscihentious that it is not Right in the Sight of god to Keep Slaves—I therefore obtain Leave of the Detachment under my Command to give the said Dinah Mattis and Nancy her Child their freedom to pass and Repass any where through the United States of America with her Behaving as becometh and to Trade and to Traffick for her Self and Child as tho' She was Born free without being Mollested by any Person or Persons.

In witness whereunto I have Set my hand or subscribed my name.

(Signed)   EBENEZE'R ALLEN *Copt."*

Manumission of Dinah Mattis and Her Daughter (1777)

Overview: Although Ebenezer Allen could have enslaved Dinah and her child or sold them for profit, he made the decision to free them, "being conscihentious that it is not Right in the Sight of god to Keep Slaves." The story of Dinah and her daughter Nancy underlines the importance of the religious abolitionism that certainly held sway among some Vermonters during the Revolutionary War.

Source: Abby M. Hemenway, ed., *The Vermont Historical Gazetteer*, 5 vols. (vol. 1: Burlington, Vt.: Miss A. M. Hemenway, 1867; vol. 2: Burlington, Vt.: Miss A. M. Hemenway, 1871; vol. 3: Claremont, N.H.: The Claremont Manufacturing Company, 1877; vol. 4: Montpelier, Vt.: Vermont Watchman and State Journal Press, 1882; vol. 5: Brandon, Vt.: Mrs. Carrie E. H. Page, 1891), 2: 580.

Head Quarters Pollett [Pawlet]

28th of November 1777

To whom it may Concern Know ye Whereas Dinah Mattis, a negro woman with nancey her Child of two months old was taken Prisnor on Lake Champlain, with the British Troops Some where near Col Gilliner's Patten the Twelth day of Instant November by a Scout under my Command, and according to a Resolve Past by the Honnorable Continental Congress that all [prizes] belong to the Captivators thereof—therefore She and her Child became the just property of the Captivators thereof—I being Conscihentious that it is not Right in the Sight of god to Keep Slaves—I therefore obtain Leave of the Detachment under my Command to give the said Dinah Mattis and Nancy her Child their freedom to pass and Repass any where through the United States of America with her Behaving as becometh and to Trade and to Traffick for her Self and Child as tho' She was Born free without being Mollested by any Person [or] Persons.

In witness whereunto I have Set my hand or subscribed my name.

Ebenezer Allen *Capt.*

Resolved, that the Representatives of this Assembly lay before their constituents the circumstances of the union subsisting between sixteen towns, on the east side of Connecticut River and the former State of Vermont; and to be instructed by them to act accordingly.

Assembly adjourned until eight o'clock, tomorrow morning.

Saturday Octr. 24th 177[8]

Assembly met, according to adjournment.

Resolved, that a Committee of three, to join a Committee from the Council be appointed to prefix the Governor's salary for the year ensuing — Committee chosen Mr. Jona. Tassett, Mr. Joshua Webb and Mr. Wells

Resolved, that a Committee of three be appointed to prepare a bill, respecting the freedom of Slaves, agreeable to the bill of rights — Committee chosen Mr. Harris, Mr. Bartley, and Mr. Cooper

(Resolved)

Legislative Committee on Slavery (1778)

Overview: This document demonstrates that the Vermont founders and the legislature realized that the 1777 abolition provision was not entirely settled law. They understood that it needed amending and clarification. Historians do not know why the committee did not prepare a bill or submit any type of legislation.

Source: Formation of a Committee to Prepare a Bill Regarding the Freedom of Slaves, October 24, 1778, Volume 1, p. 65. *Joint Assembly Journals, 1778-1965.* (A-113) A113-00001. Vermont State Archives and Records Administration, Middlesex. See also Walter H. Crockett, ed., *State Papers of Vermont,* Volume 3: *Journals and Proceedings of the General Assembly of Vermont,* part 1 (Bellows Falls, Vt.: P. H. Gobie Press, 1924), 48.

Resolved, that a Committee of three be appointed, to prepare a bill, respecting the freedom of Slaves, agreeable to the bill of rights—Committee chosen—Mr. [Edward] Harris, Mr. [Thomas] Rowley and Mr. [Thomas] Cooper——

~~judges of the spechal Court~~ maiger john Sheper-
son Judg of the spechal Court a gainst oliver
John & Elijah Louels for with holding or Secret-
ing ther Brother timoth Louels Estate one day
my Expencees 5/o ̶j̶̶̶̶̶̶̶̶̶̶̶̶̶̶̶̶̶̶   £ o-5-o
~~pompe~~ june the 22. 1778. he maid Shuer of pomp
Drake ~~&c~~ a Negro man of the Estate
timothy Louels he was in the hand of Elijah
Louel & Elijah pretended to haue a bill of Sale
of D pommp ——— my Expencees & meals — £ o-9-o
to 2 mugs. of tody — and one dram —————   o 12 o
to ~~two~~ days and a half ————————————
horse keeping ————————————————   o-4-o
J alended the sp, timSpeachel Court to be holden
westmister the
but did not Set by reason of the judges
not Coming ~~to~~ Sosistant for a Covvam was gon
three days = my Epencees ——————————   1-17-6

December the 12th 1778: Seased on 2 gilded frains
one had a map in it of Crain Brushes in the hand
of mr. Chase

J atended the Speachel Court to be Holden
at westmister the 29 of September 1778
in order for the tryel of the Louels but mr t.
weeb one of the judges who had the complaint
did not giue out a wrant a gainst them and
So nothing don = was gon thrile days ————
my Expencees ——— —— ——— ——   2-4-9

Captain Leonard Spaulding on
Pomp Brake's enslavement (1778-1779)

Overview: In the late 1770s, Pompey Brakkee (or Pomp Brake) filed a civil court case against his owner, probably for unpaid labor. The court awarded Brakkee £400. Although the court case is an example of how slaves could successfully challenge wrongful enslavement, it also shows clearly the ways in which slavery could persist after the adult abolition provision. The account book of Commissioner of Sequestration Leonard Spaulding, who oversaw the confiscation of Loyalist property, shows that Elijah Lovell of Rockingham claimed to own Brakkee despite the 1777 constitution.

Source: An Account of Leonard Spaulding [Commissioner of Sequestration], Regarding Tory estate of Timothy Lovel and a bill of sale for Pomp Brake, Volume 37, p. 26. Manuscript Vermont State Papers, 1777-1861 (series SE-118). SE118-00037. Vermont State Archives and Records Administration, Middlesex. See also Mary G. Nye, ed., *State Papers of Vermont*, Volume 6: *Sequestration, Confiscation, Sale of Estates* (Montpelier, Vt.: Rawson C. Myrick, Secretary of State, 1941), 253.

june the 22d 1778 the maid shuere of pomp Brake a Negro man of the Estate of timothy Lovels he was in the hands of Elijah Lovel Sd Elijah pretended to have a bill of Sale of sd pommp—

tempt was ever made to arrest or bring him to trial. In fact he was never engaged in any violent act whatever against the Yorkers, though it is quite probable he may have counseled resistance to the oppressive measures of New York as he afterwards did to those of the mother country. He died Dec. 24, 1778, universally lamented. He had been twice married, and left a large number of children, and has numerous descendants residing in town, who are among our most respectable inhabitants

The REV. DAVID AVERY succeeded Mr. Dewey as pastor, and was settled May 3, 1780. He had been a Chaplain in the army, and resigned that situation, when he received a call from this church. He brought with his family to town a colored woman, whom he insisted on his right to hold as a slave, which created much dissatisfaction in the church; and this, with other objections to him, occasioned his dismission at the end of three years, in May, 1783.

The REV, JOB SWIFT, D. D., was next in charge of the church and congregation, and was settled Feb. 27, 1786. He remained their pastor over sixteen years, and his labors gave great satisfaction until about the close of that time, when dissensions arising, growing out of the bitterness of party politics, he thought proper to ask a dismission, which took place June 7, 1801. He afterwards removed to Addison, in this state, and was settled over the church in that town, and died October 20, 1804, at Enosburgh, where he had gone on a mission by the consent of his people, aged 61. He was eminent as a christian and a clergyman, but as he was not a native of this town, and was not a resident here at the time of his death, this does not seem to be the place for a more extended notice of him.

After Mr. Swift left, the pulpit was supplied during a considerable portion of the years 1803 and 1804 by the Rev. Joshua Spaulding, though he was not regularly settled.

In March, 1805, the Rev. *Daniel Marsh* became the settled clergyman, and continued in charge of the church and congregation until April, 1820, when he was dismissed. He soon afterwards removed from town, and has since deceased.— He was a worthy christian minister, and enjoyed the confidence and respect of the community.

The Meeting-House had been built by voluntary subscription, and for nearly thirty years the ministers had been supported in the same manner; the method adopted to raise the sum required being, to assess the same upon the tax-lists of those who gave their assent to the contribution. But in March, 1790, an article was inserted in the warning for the town meeting, as follows, viz: "To see if the town will adopt a certain law of this State, entitled '*an act for supporting and maintaining the gospel ministry:*" and at the meeting it passed in the affirmative.

By the act thus adopted, the salary of the minister was to be assessed upon the polls and ratable estate of the inhabitants of the town, and collected in the same manner as other town taxes; and no person was to be exempt from its payment, unless he lodged with the town clerk for record, the certificate of some minister or officer of another church, that he agreed in religious sentiment with the signer thereof.

This vote created considerable dissatisfaction in the congregation, and Nathan Clark, one of the fathers of the town, denounced it in severe terms, in an article published in the Gazette, over his own signature. The practice thus initiated in 1790, of supporting the ministry by town tax, does not seem to have been abandoned until the repeal of the law on the subject in October, 1807.

The tax for the support of the Minister amounting usually to $450 per annum, appears to have been submitted to with a considerable degree of patience; but the attempt to apply the law to the building of a new Meeting-house, which would require more than a ten-fold greater tax, roused a very serious opposition. Those, however, who were in favor of thus erecting the house, were sufficiently strong to carry a vote in the town-meeting held December 12, 1803, to raise a tax of 5000 dollars for that purpose. At the same meeting a committee, consisting of Isaac Tichenor, David Robinson, Moses Robinson, jr., Thomas Abel and Jesse Field, were appointed a building committee, and the house was afterwards erected under the special superintendence of Moses Robinson, jr., the acting agent of the committee.

In 1801 the law providing for the support of the Gospel ministry, and the erection of houses of worship, was so far modified by the Legislature, that any tax-payer could be relieved from contribution, by lodging with the town clerk a certificate signed by him in the following words, viz : "I do not agree in religious opinion with a majority of the inhabitants of this town."— And soon after the vote of the meeting-house tax, the names of 136 of the payers, owning a considerable portion of the property in town, were found in the clerks's office attached to such a certificate.

When the house was completed, in December, 1805, it was found to have cost $7793,28, and that only the sum of $2200,97 had been collected of the 5000 dollars which had been assessed. It was finally agreed to sell the pews at public auction, to raise the money to pay for the house, and that persons not purchasing should have the money they had paid refunded them.

Story of a Slaveholding Bennington Minister, Vermont Historical Gazetteer (1780s)

Overview: In the early 1780s, David Avery served as a minister in Bennington. He offended local people in at least two ways. First, he did not preach what they considered an acceptable interpretation of the Gospel. Second, he openly owned a slave. As a result, the church membership forced him out. It is unclear if Avery's slaveholding was the primary reason for his eviction from the pulpit, or rather his stance on religious issues.

Source: Abby M. Hemenway, ed., *The Vermont Historical Gazetteer,* 5 vols. (vol. 1: Burlington, Vt.: Miss A. M. Hemenway, 1867; vol. 2: Burlington, Vt.: Miss A. M. Hemenway, 1871; vol. 3: Claremont, N.H.: The Claremont Manufacturing Company, 1877; vol. 4: Montpelier, Vt.: Vermont Watchman and State Journal Press, 1882; vol. 5: Brandon, Vt.: Mrs. Carrie E. H. Page, 1891), 1: 163.

The REV. DAVID AVERY succeeded Mr. Dewey as pastor, and was settled May 3, 1780. He had been a Chaplain in the army, and resigned that situation, when he received a call from this church. He brought with his family to town a colored woman, whom he insisted on his right to hold [as] a slave, which created much dissatisfaction in the church; and this, with other objections to him, occasioned his dismission [dismissal] at the end of three years, in May, 1783.

to Stake and Stones; Thence North one Hundred and
forty nine Rods to Stake and Stones in the North—west
corner of the Beam Yard; Thence West by the Highway
twenty Eight Rods to the first Mentioned bounds both
Pieces Containing fifty five Acres one hundred and one Rods
which is the third part of the Homestead.—

Also a Piece of Land lying near Mount Antoney
bought of Ithimer Hibbard as it is bounded in the Deed
Reference thereunto being Had. Also one Half of a Piece of
Land Purchased of John Rudd bounded as follows: begin
ning at Nathaniel Fillmans North—east Corner; the
South ten degrees West thirty Rods to Stake and Stones:
Thence about East to the Middle of the East Line of
Said Land about Twenty Eight Rods; Thence North ten
degrees East thirty three Rods and three quarters to Stake
and Stones; Thence West ten degrees North to the first
mentioned bounds being Sixteen Acres, Which is the one
third Part of all the Real Estate of the Said John
Armstrong Estimated at £417..10..0 Total.

The Following is the whole one third of the
Moveables belonging to the aforesaid John Armstrong
Estate Set off to His Relict.——

one Negroe Boy	£60..0..0	
one Chest of Draws	1..0..0	
one feather bed Wait 42 lb ½	4..0..0	
three Pair of Sheats at 14/ P__P	2..2..0	
two Table Cloaths at 5/ each	0..10..0	
one bedsted	0..8..0	
one bed Cord	0..2..0	
two Sets of Curtens at 10/	1..0..0	
Two Sets of Valinses	0..5..0	
one yoak of Large Oxen	14..0..0	84..7..0
one White Cow	2..14..0	
one Red and White Cow	3..0..0	
one ... Cow	3..15..0	

John Armstrong, Probate Record (1782)

Overview: This probate record demonstrates that slavery continued after the 1777 abolition provision. Several well-known Vermont politicians saw this record but did nothing to prevent this "One Negroe Boy" from continuing to be a slave for Armstrong's wife. It should be noted that the term "boy" does not necessarily mean the slave was a child. In fact, his listed price of £60 indicates that he was probably an adult.

Source: John Armstrong, Probate Record, Bennington County, 1782, Vermont Superior Court, Bennington Probate Division, Bennington.

One Negroe Boy £60

. . . .

One featherbed Wait £4

. . . .

Two Table Cloaths £0-10-0

. . . .

One Youk [yoke] of Large Oxen £14

. . . .

One White Cow £2-14[or 34?]-0
One Red and White Cow £3

Springfield ap. 3 1793

Sold to Col.n John Barrett a Negro Girl
Named Rose fourteen Years old the
fourteenth Day of Jan.y last Past, healthy
and Sound in Every Respect for the Sum
of Twenty two Pounds L. Money —

Rec.d the Contents in full ar

Pr.   Samuel Andrew

14
7
31 in 1800
18
49

BILL OF SALE, JOHN BARRETT PURCHASED ROSE FROM SAMUEL ANDREW (1783)

Overview: This bill of sale offers further evidence of the ways that slavery continued in Vermont after 1777. Although technically this sale would have been legal because of Rose's age, it is highly unlikely that Barrett intended to free her only four years after paying £22 for her services. The mathematical accounting of her age probably written by Barrett indicates that he did not intend to free her. Also, the 1791 census shows that African Americans lived in Barrett's household, but that census does not list the name and gender of all persons in a specific household.

Source: Samuel Andrew, Bill of Sale to John Barrett, April 3, 1783. Topsham John Barrett Papers, Town of Topsham, Vermont, at Special Collections, Bailey/Howe Library, University of Vermont, Burlington.

Springfield ap. 3 1783

Sold to Col. John Barrett a Negro garl Named Rose fourteen years old the fourteenth Day of [January] Last Past, healthy and Sound in Every Respect for the Sum of Twenty two Pounds [lawful] Money.

[Received] the Contents in full—
Samuel Andrew

14 in 1783
<u>17</u>
31 in 1800
<u>16</u>
49

Bill of Sale, Stephen Jacob purchased Dinah from Jotham White (1783/1801)

Overview: The case of Dinah reveals the persistence of slavery in Vermont after 1777. As a thirty-year-old woman, Dinah should have been freed by the abolition provision of the Vermont Constitution. This bill of sale brings up many questions about this female slave, including where Dinah was born,

Know all men by these presents that I Jotham White of Charlestown in the County of Cheshire and State of New Hampshire Gent.- For and in consideration of the sum of Forty Pounds lawful money to me in hand before the Delivery hereof paid by Stephen Jacob Esq. of Windsor in the County of Windsor and State of Vermont, do hereby sell and deliver to the said Stephen Jacob, my Negro Woman Slave, named Dinah, about thirty years of age.

To have and to hold the said Negro Woman Slave to the said Stephen Jacob his heirs and assigns forever, and I the said Jotham White for myself my heirs Executors and administrators do by these presents covenant and engage with the said Stephen Jacob, that I am the sole and lawful owner of the said Negro Woman and that I will Warrant and Defend the said Negro Woman Slave to him the said Stephen Jacob his heirs and assigns against the lawful Claims and Demands of all persons whatsoever. In Witness whereof I hereunto set my hand and seal this 26th Day of July anno Domini 1783

Signed Sealed and Delivered

In Presence of   Jotham White   (L.S.)

Zedekiah Stone

Isaiah Eaton

20th July 1801 I certify that the foregoing is a true copy of a bill of sale executed to me by Jotham White Esq. and consent that the same use of this copy should be made in Court as might be of the Original Instrument.

Stephen Jacob

if she married, and whether she had children. Stephen Jacob—prominent politician and eventually Vermont Supreme Court judge—and Jotham White both were familiar with the 1777 abolition provision. Yet that knowledge did not prevent them from openly flaunting the law.

Source: Jotham White, typed copy of Bill of Sale of a Negro Woman Slave, Dinah, executed to Stephen Jacob, July 26, 1783, with note appended July 20, 1801, XMS 326 W582, Vermont Historical Society, Barre. Please note that this document is a 1909 certified and typed copy of the actual 1783/1801 bill of sale. The original has been lost.

Know all men by these presents that I Jotham White of Charlestown in the County of Cheshire and State of New Hampshire Gent. — For and in consideration of the sum of Forty Pounds lawful money to me in hand before the Delivery hereof paid by Stephen Jacob Esq. of Windsor in the County of Windsor and State of Vermont, do hereby sell and deliver to the said Stephen Jacob, my Negro Woman Slave, named Dinah, about thirty years of age.

To have and to hold the said Negro Woman Slave to the said Stephen Jacob his heirs and assigns forever, and I the said Jotham White for myself my heirs Executors and administrators do by these presents covenant and engage with the said Stephen Jacob, that I am the sole and lawful owner of the said Negro Woman and that I will Warrant and Defend the said Negro Woman Slave to him the said Stephen Jacob his heirs and assigns against the lawful Claims and Demands of all persons whatsoever. In Witness whereof I hereunto set my hand and seal this 26th Day of July anno Domini 1783 Signed Sealed and Delivered

Jotham White

20th July 1801 I certify that the foregoing is a true copy of a bill of sale executed to me by Jotham White Esq. and consent that the same use of this copy should be made in Court as might be of the Original Instrument.

Stephen Jacob

Bennington 3.d Decr. 1784

D.r Sir

72

As Doct.r Huntington is Closely ingag'd in his Vocation as Physician for my brothers family Whilst Lorrain Allen is here too &c. Therefore I wish to make every ——— as payment on the part of the Doct.r as is ——— as possible, and Whereas after Collecting the note in my favour ag.t Jotham Bemus there will not be more than about one hundred dollars due you on the Note I passed to you ag.t Doct.r S. Huntington, Now if Doct.r H. aforesaid or Gen.l Ethan Allen will Satisfy you for the part of said note which is your due I will Mark said note and give you up your Re.ipt, and you will Much Oblige

D. Sir y.r Hum.l Serv.t
LEVI ALLEN.

N.B. there appears to be Some disorder in the Right Eye of the Negro fellow prince I bo.t o/ you which has been of Some time Standing, I hope it will not prove the loss of the Eye   LA

M.r Jacob A. Lansingh.

Letter of Levi Allen to Jacob Lansingh (1784)

Overview: In this letter, Levi Allen acknowledged his ownership of Prince, who accompanied him to several areas including Vermont. Allen speculated in land in East Florida and other parts of the South where slaveholding underpinned local society.

Source: Levi Allen to Jacob Lansingh, December 3, 1784. Collection of the Fort Ticonderoga Museum, Ticonderoga, New York. See also John J. Duffy, et. al., eds., *Ethan Allen and His Kin: Correspondence, 1772-1819*, 2 vols. (Hanover, N.H.: University Press of New England, 1998), 1: 164-65.

Bennington 3d. Decr. 1784
Dr. Sir.

[As] Doctr. Huntington is Closely ingaged in his vocation as a Phisian for my brothers family Lorrain Allen in particular therefore I wish to make every [. . .] payment on the part of the Doctr. as easy as possible, and whereas after collecting the note in my favour agt. Jothum Bemus there will not be more than about one hundred dollars due to you on the Note I passed to you agt. Doctr. S. Huntington, Now if Doctr. H. aforesaid or Genl. Ethan Allen will Satisfy you for the pay of Said note which is Your due I will take back Said note and give you up Your Receipt, and You will Much Oblige

D. Sir Yr. Humle. Servt.
Levi Allen

N B. there appears to be Some disorder in the Right Eye of the Negro fellow Prince I bot. of you which has been of Some time Standing, I hope it will not prove the loss of the Eye.

L A

"An Act to Prevent the Sale and Transportation of Negroes & Molattoes Out of this State" (1786)

Overview: The Sale and Transportation Act is the centerpiece of slavery studies in Vermont because it expresses the hope of the legislature to end chattel bondage in the Republic, while also acknowledging that "[i]nstances have happened of the former owners of Negroes in this Commonwealth making sale of such persons as Slaves notwithstanding their being liberated by the Constitution, and attempts have been made to transport such persons to foreign parts in open violation of the Laws of the Land." The legislation attempted to fix the loopholes left by the 1777 abolition provision by punishing those involved in trafficking black people outside of the state. However, it is not clear how the law would have been enforced.

Source: "An Act to Prevent the Sale and Transportation of Negroes & Molattos out of this State," October 30, 1786, Volume 1, p. 555. Manuscript Laws of Vermont, circa 1778-1968. (A-112). A112-00001. Vermont State Archives and Records Administration, Middlesex. See also John A. Williams, ed., *State Papers of Vermont*, Vol. 14: Laws of Vermont (Montpelier, Vt.: Harry H. Cooley, Secretary of State, 1966), 100.

Whereas by the Constitution of this State all the subjects of this Commonwealth of whatever colour are equally entitled to the inestimable blessings of Freedom unless they have forfeited the same by the commission of some crime, and the Idea of Slavery is expressly and totally exploded from our free Government.

And whereas Instances have happened of the former owners of Negroes in this Commonwealth making sale of such persons as Slaves notwithstanding their being liberated by the Constitution, and attempts have been made to transport such persons to foreign parts in open violation of the Laws of the Land.

Be it therefore enacted by the General Assembly of the State of Vermont that if any person shall hereafter make sale of any subject of this State or shall convey or attempt to convey any subject out of this State with intent to hold or sell such person as a Slave every person so offending and convicted thereof shall forfeit and pay to the person injured for such offence the sum of £100 and cost of suit to be recovered by action of debt complaint or Information.

Passed 30th Octr 1786

An Act for ascertaining the Westerly Line of Orange County and the Easterly line of Addisons County.

Be it enacted by the General Assembly of the State of Vermont that the dividing line between the Counties of Orange and Addison for the time being shall begin at the South west Corner of Kingston and thence run along the westerly lines of the towns of Roxbury, Northfield and Berlin then up Onion River about a mile and an half to the Southeasterly Corner of Middlesex then North thirty six degrees East on the west lines of Montpelier, Calais, Woodbury Hardwick and Greensborough to the Northwesterly Corner thereof and then in the most direct course on Town lines to the North — line of this State

And be it further enacted by the authority aforesaid that so much of an Act passed the sixteenth day of February 1781 entitled, an Act for the Division of Counties within this State, as fixes the line between the Counties of Orange and Addison (then Rutland) and so much of an Act passed the 21 day of February 1781 entitled, an Act for establishing the Shire or County Towns in the several Counties, and the time for holding Superior or County Courts therein, as ascertains the westerly line of Orange County be and is hereby repealed.

Passed 30th Octr 1786

An Act to prevent the Sale and transportation of Negroes & Molattoes out of this State

Whereas by the Constitution of this State all the Subjects of this Commonwealth of whatever colour are equally entitled to the inestimable blessings of Freedom unless they have forfeited the same by the commission of some crime, and the Idea of Slavery is expressly and totally exploded from our free Government.

And whereas Instances have happened of the former owners of Negroes in this Commonwealth making Sale of such persons as Slaves notwithstanding their being liberated by the Constitution, and attempts have been made to transport such persons to foreign parts in open violation of the Laws of the Land,

Be it therefore enacted by the General Assembly of the State of Vermont that if any person shall thereafter make Sale of any Subject of this State or shall convey or attempt to convey any subject out of this State with intent to hold or sell such person as a Slave every person so offending and convicted thereof shall forfeit and pay to the person injured for such offence the Sum of £100 and cost of Suit to be recovered by action of debt complaint or Information

Passed 30th Octr 1786

An Act regulating the militia of this State

For regulating the Militia of this State

Be it enacted by the General Assembly of the State of Vermont that all male persons from sixteen years of age to forty five shall constitute the Militia force of this State except members of the Council members of the house of Representatives and delegates to the Congress of the United States for the time being, the State Treasurer and Secretary of State Secretary of Council Justices of the Peace, Judges of the Supreme and County Courts, Judges of the several Probate districts auditors of the State Field Commissioned and Staff Officers Honorably discharged, Ministers of the Gospel, the President Tutors and Students of Colleges, Allowed, Physicians and Surgeons Post officers constant School Masters, one Miller to each gristmill Sheriffs Constables and Goalers, continewing Persons disabled by lameness or other bodily infirmity during the continuance of such disability producing a certificate thereof from two able Phy

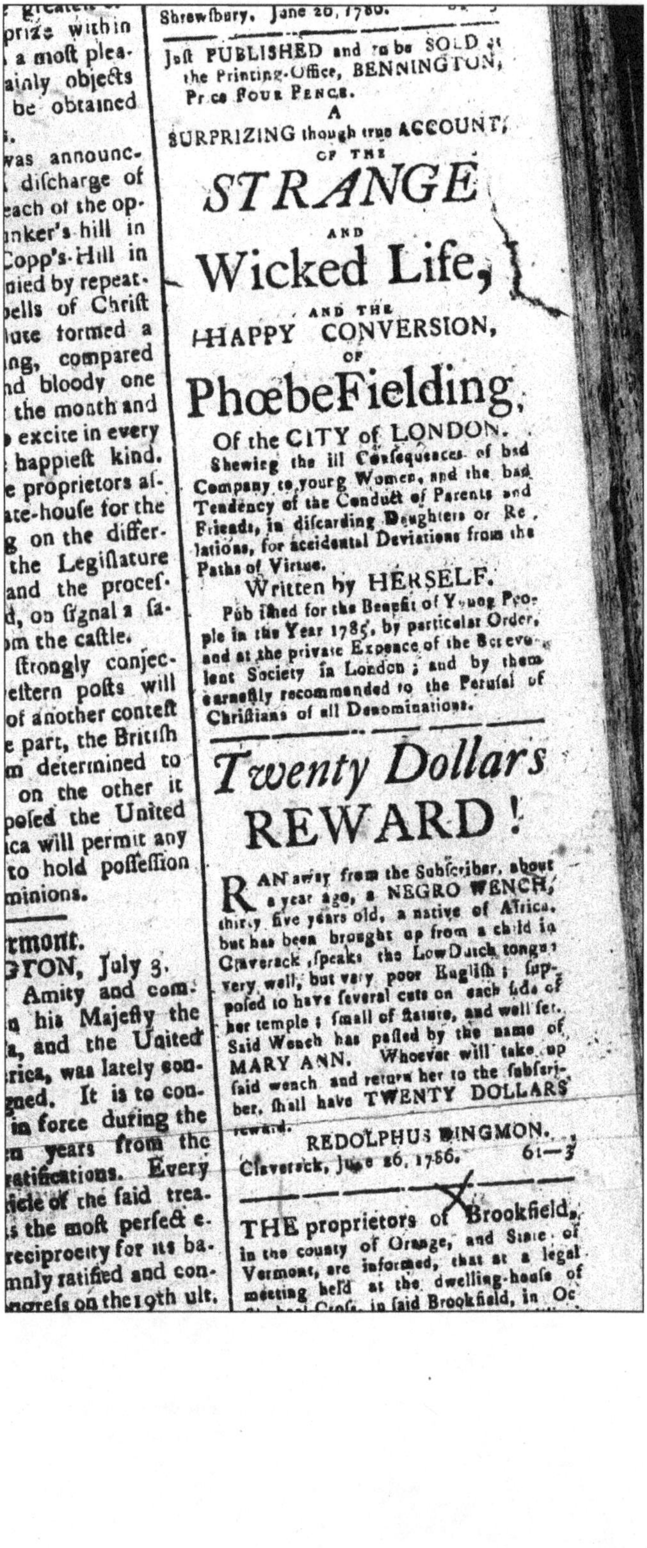

prize within
a moſt plea-
ainly objects
be obtained
.
was announc-
diſcharge of
each of the op-
nker's hill in
Copp's-Hill in
nied by repeat-
ells of Chriſt
lute formed a
ng, compared
nd bloody one
the month and
excite in every
happieſt kind.
e proprietors af-
ate-houſe for the
g on the differ-
the Legiſlature
and the procef-
d, on ſignal a fa-
om the caſtle.
ſtrongly conjec-
eſtern poſts will
of another conteſt
e part, the Britiſh
m determined to
on the other it
poſed the United
ica will permit any
to hold poſſeſſion
minions.

rmont.
GTON, July 3.
Amity and com-
n his Majeſty the
a, and the United
rica, was lately ſon-
gned. It is to con-
in force during the
n years from the
ratifications. Every
icle of the ſaid trea-
s the moſt perfect e-
reciprocity for its ba-
mnly ratified and con-
ngreſs on the 19th ult.

Shrewſbury, June 26, 1780.

Juſt PUBLISHED and to be SOLD at
the Printing-Office, BENNINGTON,
Price FOUR PENCE.
A
SURPRIZING though true ACCOUNT,
OF THE

STRANGE

AND

Wicked Life,

AND THE

HAPPY CONVERSION,

OF

PhœbeFielding,

Of the CITY of LONDON.
Shewing the ill Conſequences of bad
Company to young Women, and the bad
Tendency of the Conduct of Parents and
Friends, in diſcarding Daughters or Re-
lations, for accidental Deviations from the
Paths of Virtue.
Written by HERSELF.
Publiſhed for the Benefit of Young Peo-
ple in the Year 1785, by particular Order,
and at the private Expence of the Benevo-
lent Society in London; and by them
earneſtly recommended to the Peruſal of
Chriſtians of all Denominations.

Twenty Dollars REWARD!

RAN away from the Subſcriber, about
a year ago, a NEGRO WENCH,
thirty five years old, a native of Africa,
but has been brought up from a child in
Claverack, ſpeaks the Low Dutch tongue
very well, but very poor Engliſh; ſup-
poſed to have ſeveral cuts on each ſide of
her temple; ſmall of ſtature, and well ſet.
Said Wench has paſſed by the name of
MARY ANN. Whoever will take up
ſaid wench and return her to the ſubſcri-
ber, ſhall have TWENTY DOLLARS
reward.
REDOLPHUS DINGMON.
Claverack, June 26, 1786.   61—3

THE proprietors of Brookfield,
in the county of Orange, and State of
Vermont, are informed, that at a legal
meeting held at the dwelling-houſe of

Runaway Slave Advertisement, Vermont Gazette (1786)

Overview: Runaway slave advertisements appeared periodically in Vermont newspapers. This ad is significant for several reasons. Although born in Africa, Mary Ann must have endured the Atlantic slave trade at an extraordinarily young age because she had been raised in New York. She spoke English, Dutch, and perhaps an African language. The vast majority of runaways in colonial America were men and this trend is mirrored in the advertisements published in the *Vermont Gazette*, but Mary Ann's story shows that women also absconded from their owners. The fact that the *Gazette* published this ad well before Vermont joined the United States shows the willingness of some locals to return escaped slaves to their owners, despite the spirit if not the intent of the 1777 abolition provision. Slaveholders would not have advertised in Vermont newspapers if they had little hope that local inhabitants might help them regain escaped slaves.

Source: *Vermont Gazette*, July 3, 1786.

Twenty Dollars REWARD!
RAN away from the Subscriber, about a year ago, a NEGRO WENCH, *thirty five years old, a native of Africa, but has been brought up from a child in Claverack, speaks the Low Dutch tongue very well, but very poor English; supposed to have several cuts on each side of her temple; small of stature, and well set. Said Wench has passed by the name of* MARY ANN. *Whoever will take up said wench, and return her to the subscriber, shall have* TWENTY DOLLARS *reward.*

REDOLPHUS DINGMON
Claverack [N.Y.] June 26, 1786.

Voted, That the Dr. be admitted as a member of the Society accordingly. —

The Society took into consideration the present mode of admission of members, &c. and after mature deliberation, voted,

That a committee of three be appointed to bring in bills in form, on the following subjects, viz. —

The future mode of admission of members. — And the admission of gentlemen of the town to a participation in the library, &c. — Members chosen. Mr. J. Robinson, Mr. Timothy Follett, & Mr. A. Haswell.

Voted That the Society meet on Friday evening next, to debate on the following question, viz. (The meeting to be held at Capt. Robinson's.)

Whether it is morally or politically right for Vermont to interfere in the apprehension of Slaves escaped from other States? ~~into that State~~

Affirmative	Negative. —
J. Smith,	D. Robinson
T. Follett,	D. Fay,
N. Burr,	J. Hatheway
D. Russell.	B. Fassett,
A. Marsh	A. Haswell. —
J. Robinson	

BENNINGTON FRIENDLY SOCIETY, MINUTE BOOK, QUESTION ABOUT SLAVERY (1789)

Overview: The debate over returning slaves to their owners remained a heated topic among Vermonters in the late eighteenth century. As this vote of the Friendly Society indicates, both sides had significant support and it would be an oversimplification to see Vermont as either primarily abolitionist or in favor of returning fugitive slaves to their owners.

Source: Bennington Friendly Society, Minute Book, April 10, 1789, 57, Special Collections, Bailey/Howe Library, University of Vermont, Burlington.

Whether it is morally or politically right for Vermont to interfere in the apprehension of slaves escaped from other states?

6 Affirmative
5 Negative

Bill of Sale, Oliver Hastings purchased Anthony from Jotham White (1790)

Overview: This bill of sale is an example of child slavery that the Vermont Constitution allowed. However, after the enactment of the 1786 Transportation and Sale law, Jotham White should not have sold this young child. Significantly, we know nothing about Anthony's parents or how Jotham White obtained the boy in the first place. Although White appears to try to protect himself from any legal trouble by insisting that Anthony be freed at age 21, there would have been no way to enforce such a provision in New Hampshire, where Dr. Hastings lived. As it turns out, Oliver Hastings and Jotham White had married sisters from the same family (Reed). According to notarial records gathered by historian Marcel Trudel, Hastings sold Anthony (Antoine) to Boucherville resident Charles Boucher de Labruere for 90 bushels of wheat. (Marcel Trudel, *Dictionnaire des esclaves et de leurs proprietaries au Canada français* [Ville LaSalle: Hurtubise Cahiers du Quebec, 1990], 14.)

Source: Charles H. Hubbard and Justus Dartt, *History of the Town of Springfield, Vermont* (Boston: George H. Walker & Co., 1895), 489. I have attempted to track down the original bill of sale to no avail. I searched in various collections in Vermont, the New Hampshire Historical Society, the Charlestown (N.H.) Historical Society, and The Fort at #4, but no one seems to know what happened to the bill of sale.

[MARCH 2, 1790]

Know all men by these presents, that I, Jotham White of Springfield, in the county of Windsor and State of Vermont, gentleman, for and in consideration of the sum of thirty-five pounds in silver money to me in hand before the delivery hereof paid by Oliver Hastings of Charlestown, in the county of Cheshire and State of New Hampshire, physician, do hereby sell and deliver to the said Oliver Hastings, my negro boy slave named Anthony, about eight years and a half of age. To have and to hold the said negro boy slave to the said Oliver Hastings, his heirs and assigns, until the said negro boy shall arrive to the age of twenty-one years. I, the said Jotham White, for myself, my heirs, executors, and administrators, do by these presents covenant and engage with the said Oliver Hastings, his heirs and assigns, against the lawful claim and demands of all persons whatsoever.

JOTHAM WHITE
"Signed, sealed and delivered in presence of
AMANDA STONE.
JOEL REED."

OF SPRINGFIELD, VT. 489

The following is taken from the History of Charlestown, N. H.:

"Know all men by these presents, that I, Jotham White of Springfield, in the county of Windsor and State of Vermont, gentleman, for and in consideration of the sum of thirty-five pounds in silver money to me in hand before the delivery hereof paid by Oliver Hastings of Charlestown, in the county of Cheshire and State of New Hampshire, physician, do hereby sell and deliver to the said Oliver Hastings, my negro boy slave named Anthony, about eight years and a half of age. To have and to hold the said negro boy slave to the said Oliver Hastings, his heirs and assigns, until the said negro boy shall arrive to the age of twenty-one years. I, the said Jotham White, for myself, my heirs, executors, and administrators, do by these presents covenant and engage with the said Oliver Hastings, his heirs and assigns, against the lawful claim and demands of all persons whatsoever.

"In witness whereof I have hereunto set my hand and seal, this second day of March, in the year of our Lord seventeen hundred and ninety.

JOTHAM WHITE.

"Signed, sealed and delivered in presence of
AMANDA STONE,
JOEL REED."

NATHAN WHITE was b. in Uxbridge, Mass., March 17, 1776, and came to Springfield in the winter of 1805–6. He first located on Connecticut River, near the north line of the town, on the Townshend place. Six years later he sold this farm to Samuel Steele, and bought of Taylor Spencer the farm now owned by his son, Levi R. White, and in 1826 he moved to the meadow farm at the mouth of Black River, where he d. March 28, 1858.

In 1800 he m. Rachel Rist of Grafton, Mass., who d. May 22, 1817, aged 37. By this marriage there were ten children:

I. Sally, b. in Grafton, Mass., May 15, 1801; m. Nov. 27, 1821, Isaiah Ellis. Six children. (See Ellis family.)

II. Calvin C., b. in Grafton, Mass., Feb. 10, 1803; m. March 1, 1837, Patience A. Batchelor. They lived at Gunplain, Mich., and had five children. He d. Nov. 8, 1880.

III. Luther, b. in Grafton, Mass., Oct. 24, 1804; m. Jan. 23, 1826, Fanny Glazier.

IV. Eliza Ann, b. in Springfield, Aug. 31 1806; m. Nov. 2, 1823, Jonas B. Spencer, d. May 10, 1834. (See Spencer family.)

V. Caroline, b. in Springfield, March 29, 1808; m. Dec. 25, 1831, Daniel Tower, d. in Michigan, October, 1846.

VI. Elias, b. in Springfield, Nov. 27, 1810; d. unm.

VII. Sophia, b. in Springfield, July 8, 1812; m. Jan. 23, 1834, Lewis Weston; he d. Dec. 2, 1869.

DOCUMENT 15

FEDERAL CENSUS FOR VERMONT (1791)

Overview: This document shows the number of people of African descent living in Vermont the year it joined the Union as the fourteenth state. The status of black people as free or enslaved is ambiguous, and there is evidence that the 1791 census, and later ones, undercounted African Americans in Vermont. For example, the Jacob and Barrett households both contained slaves in the early 1790s, but the census listed the black people in their homes as free. It is also important to note the surprising number of African Americans living in certain white households. For example, ten black people lived with Henry Cole in Brattleboro. The actual nature of their relationship to one another or to Henry Cole is not clear from the census data.

Source: *Heads of Families at the First Census of the United States Taken in the Year 1790, Vermont* (Washington, D.C.: Government Printing Office, 1907).

8   FIRST CENSUS OF THE UNITED STATES.

Population of the United States as returned at the First Census, by states: 1790.

DISTRICT.	Free white males of 16 years and upward, including heads of families.	Free white males under 16 years.	Free white females, including heads of families.	All other free persons.	Slaves.	Total.
Vermont	22,435	22,328	40,505	255	[1]16	[2]85,539
New Hampshire	36,086	34,851	70,160	630	158	141,885
Maine	24,384	24,748	46,870	538	None.	96,540
Massachusetts	95,453	87,289	190,582	5,463	None.	378,787
Rhode Island	16,019	15,799	32,652	3,407	948	68,825
Connecticut	60,523	54,403	117,448	2,808	2,764	237,946
New York	83,700	78,122	152,320	4,654	21,324	340,120
New Jersey	45,251	41,416	83,287	2,762	11,423	184,139
Pennsylvania	110,788	106,948	206,363	6,537	3,737	434,373
Delaware	11,783	12,143	22,384	3,899	8,887	[3]59,094
Maryland	55,915	51,339	101,395	8,043	103,036	319,728
Virginia	110,936	116,135	215,046	12,866	292,627	747,610
Kentucky	15,154	17,057	28,922	114	12,430	73,677
North Carolina	69,988	77,506	140,710	4,975	100,572	393,751
South Carolina	35,576	37,722	66,880	1,801	107,094	249,073
Georgia	13,103	14,044	25,739	398	29,264	82,548
Total number of inhabitants of the United States exclusive of S. Western and N. territory	807,094	791,850	1,541,263	59,150	694,280	3,893,635

	Free white males of 21 years and upward.	Free males under 21 years of age.	Free white females.	All other persons.	Slaves.	Total.
S. W. territory. N. "	6,271	10,277	15,365	361	3,417	35,691

[1] The census of 1790, published in 1791, reports 16 slaves in Vermont. Subsequently, and up to 1860, the number is given as 17. An examination of the original manuscript returns shows that there never were any slaves in Vermont. The original error occurred in preparing the results for publication, when 16 persons, returned as "Free colored," were classified as "Slave."

[2] Corrected figures are 85,425, or 114 less than figures published in 1790, due to an error of addition in the returns for each of the towns of Fairfield, Milton, Shelburne, and Williston, in the county of Chittenden; Brookfield, Newbury, Randolph, and Strafford, in the county of Orange; Castleton, Clarendon, Hubbardton, Poultney, Rutland, Shrewsbury, and Wallingford, in the county of Rutland; Dummerston, Guilford, Halifax, and Westminster, in the county of Windham; and Woodstock, in the county of Windsor.

[3] Corrected figures are 59,096, or 2 more than figures published in 1790, due to error in addition.

Overall

All other free persons: 255
Slaves: 16
Total African American Population: 271 [the census undercounted free African Americans]
Total Population: 85,539

Black Population in Vermont Counties

Addison: 37
Bennington: 33
Chittenden: 23
Orange: 41
Rutland: 32
Windham: 58
Windsor: 45
Total: 269 [the census lists 271 total]

Individual Households

Head of Household: Stephen Jacob
Location: Windsor
All other free persons: 2

Head of Household: John Barrett
Location: Springfield Town
All other free persons: 2

Head of Household: Henry Cole
Location: Brattleboro
All other free persons: 10

Head of Household: Jonathan Saxton
Location: Ferrisburgh
All other free persons: 9

Head of Household: John Stroud
Location: Dummerston
All other free persons: 10

12   FIRST CENSUS OF THE UNITED STATES.

ADDISON COUNTY—Continued.

NAME OF HEAD OF FAMILY.	Free white males of 16 years and upward, including heads of families.	Free white males under 16 years.	Free white females, including heads of families.	All other free persons.	Slaves.
CORNWALL TOWN—con.					
Campbell, James	1	1	4		
Tomblin, Stephen	2		5		
Squier, Wait	1	1	1		
Squier, Timothy	1		3		
Hall, Benjᵐ	1		1		
Hall, Reuben	1		2		
Gibbs, Henry	1	1	5		
Scovil, Daniel	1		2		
Douglass, Rhoda	1	1	1		
Fields, Elisha	1	1	2		
Rockwell, John	2	2	4		
Wright, Elisha	1	2	3		
Wright, Elisha	1		1		
Mead, Isaac	1		1		
Mead, Ezra	2		2		
Rockwell, John, Jr	2	2	5		
Ives, Enos	2		1		
Prat, David	1	2	1		
Ives, Enos, Jur	1	1	2		
Nutting, David	2	3	5		
Dilleno, Nathan	1	1	5		
Dilleno, Abisha	2	4	3		
Chapman, Lemuel	1	1	2		
Newell, Ebenezer	2	3	4		
Richardson, Barzill	1	3	3		
Minor, Richard	1		6		
Jarus, Israel C	3	1	1		
Ballard, John	2	1	2		
Reeves, Benjamin	2	1	6		
Newell, Riverus	1	2	6		
Sampson, Daniel	1	1	1		
Mead, Caizah	1		3		

NAME OF HEAD OF FAMILY.	Free white males of 16 years and upward, including heads of families.	Free white males under 16 years.	Free white females, including heads of families.	All other free persons.	Slaves.
FERRISBURG TOWN—continued.					
Saxton, Jonathan	1	1	4	9	
Odle, John	1	1	5		
Hawley, Gidion	2	3	2		
Chilson, Joseph	1		1		
Burrus, Joseph	2	1	3		
Tupper, Absolum	2	2	4		
Powers, Joseph	1	3	4		
Tompson, Abel	2		4		
Drewey, Noble	1		1		
Olford, Bennedick	1	1	2		
Akins, James	1	1	1		
Barnes, Joshua	1	2	2		
Barnes, Richard	1		1		
Chase, Abraham	6	2	7		
Davies, Daniel	3	1	4		
Dakins, Timothy	1	1	1		
Dakins, Presarvid	1	4	3		
Fields, Anthoney	5	1	3		
Fuller, Ashbel	1	3	1		
Fields, John	1	3	1		
Goodridg, James	2	1	1		
Fuller, Ishem	1	4	2		
Gage, George	2	2	4		
Gage, Warler	1	5	2		
Gage, William, Ju	1	4	5		
Hoyegg, Eligah	2		2		
Hatch, Jeremiah	2		1		
Hoff, John	1	5	2		
Huntley, John	1		2		
Jacobs, Lewis	1	2	3		
Keetor, Jonathan	4	1	3		
Kellogg, William	3	1	3		

NAME OF HEAD OF FAMILY.	Free white males of 16 years and upward, including heads of families.	Free white males under 16 years.	Free white females, including heads of families.	All other free persons.	Slaves.
LEICESTER TOWN.					
Merrifield, Joseph	3	2	1		
Powers, Blanchard	1	1	4		
Mack, Robert	2	1	3		
Cook, Nathaniel	1	1	2		
Cook, Elkanah	1		3		
Sawyer, Stephen	1	1	3		
Porry, Abijah	2	1	2		
Brigham, Abner	1	1	2		
Moore, George	1		1		
Olin, Henry	2	1	6		
Swinnington, Joseph	1	1	1		
Reed, Isaac	2		2		
Whitman, Benjᵐ	1	3	3		
Rounds, Wᵐ	1		2		
Childs, Ebenezer	1		1		
Dagget, John	2	2	3		
Farr, Salmon	1	2	4		
Dow, James	4	1	3		
Swinnington, James	1	1	5		
Sparks, Stephen	1	3	3		
Fish, David	1	2	4		
Smith, John	2	4	1		
Chapman, Nathaniel	1		2		
Capron, Joseph	1		3		
Griswold, Moses	2	1	6		
Church, Caleb	1	2	4		
Church, Silas	1		1		
Bacon, Jacob	1	1	2		
Bacon, Asa	2	5	4		
Whitman, John	1	3	4		
Lawson, John	1	1	2		
Dow, Moses	1	5	2		

Petition for Compensation for Support of an Invalid Foreign Negro (1791)

Overview: The high cost of caring for John Johnson led the Vermont Assembly to attempt to pass the Negro and Mulatto Act of 1791. Johnson's high medical costs upset many frugal Vermonters who worried that runaway slaves or poor free blacks would become public charges.

Source: Selectmen of Rutland Petition for Compensation for Care Given by Town to a Sick Negro, a Foreigner, 1791, Volume 18, p. 234. Manuscript Vermont State Papers, 1777-1861 (series SE-118). SE118-00018. Vermont State Archives and Records Administration, Middlesex. See also Edward A. Hoyt, ed., *State Papers of Vermont, Volume 9, General Petitions, 1788-1792* (Montpelier, Vt.: Howard E. Armstrong, Secretary of State, 1955), 281-282.

To the [Honorable] General Assembly of the State of Vermont Now Conven'd at Bennington

The Petition of Samuel Williams & William Barr Select Men for the Town of Rutland in the County of Rutland in Behalf of sd Town Humbly Sheweth, That in the Month of February 1789 One John Johnson a Negro man Came Into Sd Town of Rutland in a Sick Lame & Suffering Condition With a Lameness on One of his Thys having Ten or Twelve Lerge Runing Sores between his Knee & his Hip Dischargeing Lerge quantities of Peutred Matter being Painfull Offencive & Troublesome, and in his helpless & Suffering Condition from Princepals of Humanity Was Taken under the Care of the Select men of sd Town of Rutland and hath Ever Since ben under their Care at the Expence of sd Town of Rutland With the Constant Expence of Surgeons Nurses & attendance, in a helpless Condition to the Present Time—That the Sd John Johnson is not an Inhabitant or native of This or the United States but Was a Soldier in the French army in America the Late War, and a Native of [Saint Domingo] – and on his becoming Chargable,

by Statute Law of this State hath become an Expence to the State, and from which Sd Town of Rutland Aught to be Reliev'd…
Dated Rutland, Jany 12th, 1791

Samuel Williams
William Barr

An Act in addition to an Act intitled „ An Act providing for, and Ordering transient, Idle, impotent, & poor persons

Whereas Divers Negroes Molattoes and persons held to Service in Other States & Kingdoms under the Laws of Such State or Kingdoms frequently Escape from their Masters or owners and Run into this State and Doubts have arisen whither they be not thereby discharged from Such Service or Labour—

It is hereby Enacted by the General Assembly of the State of Vermont that the master or owner of any Negroe Molattoe or of any person whatsoever held to Service or Labor in any of the United States or in any Kingdom or State under the Laws and by the authority of the same ~~which~~ have or may hereafter Escape into this State be and are hereby impowered peaceably to take Such Negroe Molattoe or person thus held to Service as aforsaid and the Same to Convey to the place from whence they Escaped and if any person or persons whatsoever Shall impede or hinder any Such Master or owner from so taking his Negroe Molattoe or person held to Service or Labor as aforsaid or Shall Rescue such Negroe Molattoe or person held to Service as aforsaid when taken by his Master or owner and be thereof Convicted Shall for Every Such Offence forfeit & pay to such Master or owner the Sum of Eight pounds Lawful Money to be recovered by Action Plaint or Information ——

And be it further Enacted by the authority aforsaid that when such Master or owner of any Such Negroe Molattoe or person held to Service or Labor as aforsaid Shall Deem it Necessary to Call to his assistance the Civil power upon Complaint made by Such Master or owner to any Justice of the peace — and producing Satisfactory Evidence to such Justice that he is intitled to the Service or Labor of such Negroe Molattoe or person held to Service or Labor as aforsaid such Justice Shall by warrant Cause such Negroe Molattoe or person held to Service or Labor as aforsaid to be apprehended and Delivered up to be removed to the State or Kingdom from whence he Escaped and all Cost arising thereon Shall be paid by Such Master or owner

NEGRO AND MOLATTO ACT (1791)

Overview: The 1791 Negro and Molatto Act would have enforced the return of escaped slaves to their owners, but it also was designed to drastically reduce the rights of free black Vermonters. Although the Assembly rejected the bill, 31% of the legislators supported it. The Negro and Molatto Act attempted to strip free Afro-Vermonters of the most basic rights and threatened to fine local inhabitants for helping escaped slaves. The act would have allowed town selectmen to indenture free blacks to hard labor if they appeared "indolent, vicious, or likely to become chargeable to the public."

Source: "An Act to enable the masters of slaves or servants who escape from them, to apprehend such slaves or servants, and carry them out of this state and to enable the selectmen of the several towns of this state to bind out to service such free negroes as appear to them indolent, vicious, or likely to become chargeable to the public, Act Respecting Negr[oes] & Molattoes," January 24, 1791, Volume 3, page 80. Manuscript Vermont State Papers, 1777-1861 (series SE-118). SE118-00003. Vermont State Archives and Records Administration, Middlesex. See also Walter H. Crockett, ed., *State Papers of Vermont*, vol. 3, part 4: *Journals and Proceedings of the State of Vermont* (Bellows Falls: The Wyndham Press, 1929), 225.

Whereas Diverse Negroes, Molattoes, and persons held to Service in Other States & Kingdoms under the Laws of Such State or Kingdoms frequently Escape from their Masters or Owners and Run into this State and Doubts have arisen whither they are not thereby discharged from such Service or Labor.

It is hereby enacted by the General Assembly of the State of Vermont that the master or owner of any Negroe Molattoe or of any person whatsoever held to Service or Labor in any of the United States or in any Kingdom or State under the Laws and by the authority of the Same which have or may hereafter escape into this State be and are hereby impowered personally[?] to take such Negroe Molattoe or person thus held to Service as aforesaid and the Same to Convey to the place from whence they escaped and if any person or person whatsoever shall impede or hinder any such Master or Owner from taking his Negroe Molattoe or persons Held to Service or labor as aforesaid or shall rescue such Negroe Molattoe or person held to Service as aforesaid when taken by his Master or Owner and be thereof Convicted shall for Every Such Offence forfeit & pay to such Master or Owner the sum of Eight pounds Lawful Money....

And be it further Enacted by the Authority aforesaid that when such Master or Owner of any such Negroe Molattoe or person held to Service or labor as aforesaid shall Deem it Necessary to call to his assistance the Civil power upon complaint made by such Master or owner to any Justice of the peace—and producing Satisfactory Evidence to such Justice that he is entitled to the Service or Labor of such Negroe Molattoe or person held to Service or Labor as aforesaid such Justice shall by warrant cause such Negroe Molattoe or person held to Service or Labor as aforesaid to be apprehended and Delivered up to be removed to the State or Kingdom from whence he Escaped and all cost arising thereon Shall be paid by such Master or Owner.

And the more Effectually [?] to prevent Negroes & Molattoes from Strolling from town to town as idle Vagrants.

Be it Further Enacted by the Authority aforesaid that if any Negro or Molattoe Shall be found Strolling from Town to Town or from one place to another as an Idle Vagabond it shall be in the power of any one justice of the peace or Select Man of Such Town where Such Negroe or Molattoe Shall come or be found to warn such Negroe or Molattoe to depart this State within Thirty Days and if such Negroes or Molattoe Shall after the Expiration of thirty Days from his being thus warned as aforesaid be found within this State as an Idle Vagrant it may & shall be lawfull for the Select Men or a Majority of those [them?] in the Town where such Negroe or Molattoe Shall be found after the expiration of the said Thirty Days as aforesaid to apprehend such Negroe or Molattoe and by indenture to bind out to hard Service or Labor Such Negroe or Molattoe Not Exceeding Three years and the person or Persons to whom such Negroe or Molattoe shall be thus bound be and are hereby declared to have a property in the Service or Labor of such Negroe or Molattoe and all money arising from the service or labor of such Negro or Molattoe excepting such as shall be necessary to make such Negro or Molattoe Comfortable shall be by such Select Men applied to the Suport of the poor provided nevertheless that if such Negroe or Molattoe after being warned as aforesaid can within the said thirty Days procure one or more good & sufficient freeholder to be bound before any one Justice of the Peace in a bond of two Hundred pounds, to the treasurer of the

State Conditioned that such Negroe or Molattoe shall not become a cost or Charge to this State or to any Town or Corporation therein and obtain from such Justice a certificate there of such Negro or Molattoe shall not be liable to be bound in Service & it shall be the Duty of such Justice to return such bond [to the state].

Provided also that if such Negro or Molattoe can in [a] lawful town Meeting in any town in this State procure such Meeting to vote him an inhabitant of that particular town he shall not be liable to be bound in service as aforesaid but such Town voting him an inhabitant as aforesaid shall be liable to support him if such Negro or Molattoe should come to want—

And the more effectually to carry into Execution this act be it further Enacted by the Authority aforesaid that when any Negro or Molattoe shall by reason of age, sickness, or otherwise become unable to provide for himself such Negro or Molattoe shall be provided for & Supported at the Charge & Expense of such Town where Such Negro or Molattoe last resided unless Such Town can find estate of such Negroe or Molattoe or Relations or Master who by Law are obliged to Support Such Negro or Molatto.

And be it further enacted by the authority aforesaid that an act Intitled an Act to Prevent the Sale & Transportation of Negroes and Molattoes Out of this State passed October 30, 1786 be and hereby is repealed.

atriots, and a-
ists. The lat-
d Carpentras,
oo men, was
ps. On the
s proposed by

ED STATES.

of the 22nd
umane soci-
the effects
hey seem to
n the use of
to doctor
re the phi-
some years
e read. I
s the only
ay not be
laudanum
death that
ter, in cer-

Philadel-
had died
a friend's
ent thro'
; I was
ais to be
ned from
acquaint-
r, I took
a very
ne jill;
most in-
so vio-
through
uld not
ppened
y drank
h—in a
ceeded.
in, or
g.

A common interest with his constituents.

2. A general acquaintance with their interests and feelings.

3. He should be a man of integrity, firmness and honor.

4. He should have information, and talents to communicate that information with ease and propriety.

5. He should sustain the character of being faithful to his employers and persevering in his measures; not easily diverted from his course. The pilot, who veers about with every gust of wind, will inevitably endanger the ship.

6. He should however have wisdom to direct and candor to influence him in every measure.

7. He should be able to remember where he came from and to know where he has got to.

Should any man without proper qualifications procure himself to be elected, I will venture to predict that he within two years will find himself in a very public place without his breeches.

VATES.

FIVE POUNDS REWARD.

RAN away from the subscriber, in Ballstown, on the sixteenth instant, a negro man named BILL. said negro is a stout well built fellow, supposed to be between forty and fifty years old, had on when he went away a tow shirt and trowsers, wool hat, and shoes. He calls himself a doctor, and has formerly followed that business in Shaftsbury and Arlington, in the state of Vermont. Said negro was formerly owned by capt. Mead in Stillwater, but is now the property of the subscriber. Whoever will take up and secure said negro, so that the owner can get him again shall receive the above reward by me.
STEPHEN BALL.

Ballstown, July, 16 1791.

WHEREAS application hath been made to me the subscriber, by more than one sixteenth part of the proprietors of the township of Leicester, in the county of Addison, and state of Vermont, to notify and warn a meeting of said proprietors. These are therefore to notify and warn said proprietors to meet at the dwellinghouse of col. Thomas Sawyer, in said Leicester, on the third Thursday of August next, at ten o'clock in the forenoon, to act on the following articles. First, To choose a moderator to govern said meeting. Second, A proprietor's clerk and other officers that may be necessary in said propriety. Third, To see whether the proprietors will ratify the former proceedings of said proprietors, or such part of them as they shall think necessary, or set them aside. Fourth, To see whether they will divide the whole or any part of the land in said town, into divisions, and make surveys accordingly. Fifth, To grant a tax if necessary, and to do any other business proper to be done at said meeting.

St. Johns

APPLIC
subscri
proprietors of
and state of P
etors. These a
dwellinghouse o
21st day of Oc
then and there t
if the proprieto
the proprietors
committee. 3.
rectify and comp
the proprietors t
all demands agai
rited pitches. 5
demands, and an
sary when met.

Guildhall, Ju

THE propri
LUDLO
of Vermont, who
of one penny on t
public rights excep
their session in W
the expence of men
bridges through sai
a proportion of the
the house of mr. J
second Monday of S
forenoon, as will p
by previous payment
low:

David Austin,
Nathaniel Penfield
Nathaniel Fellows
Eliakim Hall, jun.
Amos Lee,
John Mix
Charles Norton
John Newell
Samuel Hitchcock
Samuel Bishop, jun.
Jared Lee
Josiah Newell
Uri Tuttle
John Dickerson
Isaac Doolittle
George Hensdale

DOCUMENT 18

Runaway Slave Advertisement, Vermont Gazette (1791)

Overview: This runaway advertisement is fascinating because it notes that Bill followed the profession of doctor in Vermont. The document also reveals that he had multiple owners.

Source: *Vermont Gazette*, July 25, 1791.

FIVE POUNDS REWARD.
RAN away from the subscriber, in Ballstown, on the sixteenth instant, a negro man named BILL. Said negro is a stout well built fellow, supposed to be between forty and fifty years old, had on when he went away a tow shirt and trowsers, wool hat, and shoes. He calls himself a doctor, and has formerly followed that business in Shaftsbury and Arlington, in the State of Vermont. Said negro was formerly owned by capt. Mead in Stillwater, but is now the property of the sub-scriber. Whoever will take up and secure said negro, so that the owner can get him again shall receive the above reward by me.

STEPHEN BALL
Bal[l]stown, [N.Y.] July 16, 1791.

mmanded by M.
29 battalions of
guards, and 48

manded by M.
talions of regu-
& 54 squadrons.
regulars,
al guards,
horse,
rovision horses.
ional guards—
rve.)

July 27.
his flourishing
inced by the
tants, than by
nd vegetables
scarce a day
ork, mutton,
nd the fruits
ur doors in
easing expec-
, when fast
, Bennington
most country
ay never-fa-
wealth; and
the honest

of mr. Eli-
imbing the
some hens
to the floor,
gree as to
ur.
senator of
Newhamp-
te.

g in Nor-
our wom-
ngest of

themselves with the patronage of the public—and flatter
that those who call will not often be disappointed in
the article required, or displeased at the price.
Scarce any thing is refused in payment at said store.
27th July, 1792.
9tf

FORTY DOLLARS REWARD.

RAN away from the subscriber, on the night of
the 26th of June last, two negro men, one
named JACK, and the other Dick; they are each
about twenty years of age; Jack is about
five feet ten inches high, and Dick is about one inch
shorter; Jack is a stout well built fellow, very black,
and full faced; he carried with him two blue cloth
coats, one was new; one french coat, sailor's jacket
and a westcoat, of home made cloth; one pair of
breeches of striped cloth; also, a striped westcoat,
both new together, with two pair of tow cloth
trowsers, and four pair of stockings.
Dick is not very black, and much freckled in the
face; he has a very singular mark on the outside of
one of his legs, occasioned by a horse newly shod
jumping on it, which has left the mark of two horse
shoes; he had on when he went away, an old shirt
and trowsers of tow cloth, a new high crowned felt
hat, and a pair of velvet breeches and westcoat.—
Both of them speak English, and Dutch, very well.

JOHN KNICKERBACER,
of Scaghticook.
HARMAN VAN VEIGHTN,
of Pittstown.
Renssalear County, July 17, 1792.
9—1

WE the subscribers, being appointed by the honorable court of probate, for the district of Fairha-
ven, commissioners, to examine the claims of the creditors
to the estate of Jonathan Frances, late of Wells, deceased, represented insolvent, hereby give notice—That they
will attend to the business of their appointment, on the
first Wednesdays of September, October, and November
next, at the house of captain Abel Merriman, in said
Wells, from one o'clock afternoon to six on each of said
days. No accounts will be allowed unless properly attested, to

WILLIAM POTTER,
JOSEPH LOVETT.
Wells, July 19th, 1792.
9—1

THE proprietors of Hinesburgh, in the county of
Chittenden, and state of Vermont, are hereby no-
tified—That at a legal adjourned meeting of said proprietors, holden in said Hinesburgh, on the 7th day of June
inst. a tax was voted of four shillings on each proprietor's right. (public rights excepted) in

lings and
etor's righ
of paying
roads, and
proportion
twelve set
shillings a
ing commi
the said tax
me the sub
ately, their
directs.
Likewise
dollar tax,
scriber, or t
law directs.
Guildhall.

WHER
the township of
of Vermont, to
is therefore to
town, to meet
in said Topsham
11 o'clock a. m
moderator and
prietors on their
ana, if they th
confirm any acts
they stand record
person who acted
keeping of Danie
allotment and sev
to a survey and p
lard. 3d. To cho
and empowered for
To confer with an
bordering on said
tween them, in
respecting such line
—Also, at the exp
maintain, or defen
which may depend
er in any way conce
tors.—To settle wit
whose land may be
alteration of any of
ing to him or them
said town, or other
convey, or in any wa
prietors] all or any p
in said township

Runaway Slave Advertisement, Vermont Gazette (1792)

Overview: These two slaves, Jack and Dick, absconded from their owners together. Both men spoke Dutch and English fluently, like most slaves in the upstate New York/Vermont region.

Source: *Vermont Gazette*, July 27, 1792.

FORTY DOLLARS REWARD.
RAN away from the subscriber, on the night of the 26th of June last, two negro men, one named JACK, and the other Dick; they are each of them about twenty years of age; Jack is about five feet ten inches high, and Dick is about one inch shorter; Jack is a stout well built fellow, very black, and full faced; he carried with him two blue cloth coats, one was new; one french coat, sailor's jacket and a westcoat, of home made cloth; one pair of breeches of striped cloth; also, a striped westcoat, both new together, with two pair of tow cloth trowsers, and four pair of stockings.

Dick is not very black, and much freckled in the face; he has a very singular mark on the outside of one of his legs....he had on when he went away, an old shirt and trowsers of tow cloth, a new high crowned felt hat, and a pair of velvet breeches and westcoat.—Both of them speak English, and Dutch, very well.

JOHN KNICKERBACER
of Scaghticook
HARMAN VAN VEIGHTN
of Pittstown
Renssalear County, [N.Y.] July 17, 1792.

ley's Fables, Lady's Library, Gregory's Legacy,
School for Scandal, Bradley's, Nile's, Robbin's
Dwight's, Emmon's, Hopkin's, and Spring's Sermons.

List of letters remaining in the Post-Office.

JOHN BUCK, Manchester or Shaftsbury, Verm.
Nathan Weller, Danby,
Mr. Remington, Rupert,   Do.
Messrs. Charles Wood and Co. Manchester, Do.
                          ABEL ALLIS, D. P. M.
Manchester, Oct. 1, 1792.
                                             1—3

Fifteen Dollars Reward.

RUN away from the subscriber, on the 1st of
Oct. inst. a NEGRO MAN, named A-
MOS, about twenty-two years of age, had on when
he went away, a French coat, made of light coloured broadcloth, lappelled, a pair of olive coloured
fustian overalls, a high crowned felt hat, and a striped
jacket with two rows of white buttons. He is supposed to be in some part of the state of Vermont, as
he formerly resided with Mr. Simon Tull, at Arlington. His complexion is remarkably black, and his
legs are more than commonly crooked; he is full-
faced, and is about 5 feet ten inches high, in his behaviour he is naturally very civil, and expresses himself in English or Dutch with considerable propriety.
Any person or persons who will apprehend the aforesaid negro man, and will deliver him to the subscriber
at Scaghticook-point, in the county of Ransler, in
the state of Newyork, shall be entitled to the above
reward, payable on demand, by me,
                          LODEWECUS VICLE.
October 10th, 1792.
                                             1—3

Runaway Slave Advertisement, Vermont Gazette (1792)

Overview: Amos escaped from his master in New York (Lodewecus Viole, or Lodowick Veile) and tried to return to Vermont, where he had lived with a man named Simon Tull in Arlington. Amos's relationship to this man is not clear. Did he formerly work for Tull, or did Tull possibly own him? Amos's master described him as "naturally very civil" with an ability to express himself with "considerable propriety."

Source: *Vermont Gazette*, October 19, 1792.

Fifteen Dollars Reward.
RUN away from the subscriber, on the 1st of Oct. inst., a NEGRO MAN, named AMOS, about twenty-two years of age, had on when he went away, a French coat, made of light coloured broadcloth, lapelled, a pair of olive coloured sustian overalls, a high crowned felt hat, and a striped jacket with two rows of white buttons. He is supposed to be in some part of the state of Vermont, as he formerly resided with Mr. Simon Tull, at Arlington. His complexion is remarkably black, and his legs are more than commonly crooked; he is full-faced, and is about 5 feet ten inches high, in his behaviour he is naturally very civil, and expresses himself in English or Dutch with considerable propriety. Any person or persons who will apprehend the aforesaid negro man, and will deliver him to the subscriber at Scaghticookpoint, in the county of Ransler, in the state of Newyork, shall be entitled to the above reward, payable on demand, by me,

LODEWECUS VIOLE. [Lodowick Veile]
October 10th, 1792.

An Act for regulating and governing the Militia of the
State of Vermont and for repealing all laws heretofore passed for that purpose —

Whereas the laws for the regulating and governing the
Militia of this State have become too complicate for practice and by reason of the several alterations which have
been from time to time made therein — Therefore,

I It is hereby Enacted by the General Assembly of the
State of Vermont that the several laws heretofore made for
governing and regulating the Militia of this State be and
hereby are repealed — Provided nevertheless, that all
officers actually in commission agreeably to the laws which
are hereby repealed, and in grades which are established
by this Act (excepting field officers who are by this act
declared to be deranged) shall continue in commission
in the same manner and in the same authority they
would in case the said laws were still in force — and all suits
depending in any court by force of said laws, shall and
may be prosecuted to final judgment and execution — And

II It is hereby further Enacted that each and every ca-
pable bodied white male citizen of this or any other of the
United States residing within this State, who is, or shall
be of the age of sixteen years (except as is hereinafter
excepted) shall severally and respectively be subject to
the requisitions of this act, and shall be enrolled in the
Militia by the captain or commanding officer of the company within whose bounds such citizen shall reside, within
three months from and after the passing this act — and it shall
be at all times hereafter the duty of the commanding officer of such company to enroll every such citizen as aforesaid, and also those who shall from time to time arrive at
the age of sixteen years or being of the age of sixteen
years and under the age of forty five years and not herein after excepted, shall come to reside within his bounds,
and shall without delay notify such citizen of the enrol-
ment by a non-commissioned officer or other person duly
authorized for that purpose by whom such notice may be
proved — And in all cases of doubt respecting the age of any
person enrolled or intended to be enrolled the party question-
ed shall prove his age to the satisfaction of the commanding officer of the company within whose bounds he may
reside — Provided always that no non-commissioned offi-

MILITIA ACT (1793)

Overview: The revised Militia Act of 1793 required all enlistments to be "white male" citizens of Vermont or the United States. In contrast, the Militia Act of 1787 did not have any such racial qualification. It simply noted that "all male persons" ages 16 to 45 could join the militia. Certainly, black soldiers had served respectably in Vermont regiments during the Revolutionary War.

97

Source: "An Act for Regulating and Governing the Militia of the State of Vermont and for Repealing All Laws Heretofore Passed for the Purpose," October 29, 1793, Volume 3, p. 49. Manuscript Laws of Vermont, circa 1778-1968. (A-112). A112-00003. Vermont State Archives and Records Administration, Middlesex. See also John A. Williams, ed., *State Papers of Vermont*, Volume 15: *Laws of Vermont* (Montpelier, Vt.: Harry H. Cooley, 1967), 211.

It is hereby further Enacted That each and every free able bodied white male citizen of this or any other of the United States residing within this State, who is, or shall be of the age of sixteen years (except as is hereinafter excepted) shall severally and respectively be subject to the requisitions of this act, and shall be enrolled in the Militia by the captain or commanding officer of the company within whose bounds such citizens shall reside, within three months from and after the passing [of] this act.

ere.

My friends have liberty to make what ufe they pleafe
my letters ; but if they think proper to publifh them,
extracts from them, I expect they will do me the
ftice to publifh the author's name.

I am fir, your humble fervant,
WILLIAM EATON, Capt. 4th U. S.
Sub Legion.
Lieut, JAMES UNDERHILL,
Commandant at the recruiting ren-
dezvous in Bennington.

P. S. The printers, who have amufed themfelves
n publifhing the extract, will, I truft, be generous
hough to gratify me by publifhing your explana-
ons.

To whom it may concern.

This certifies that Captain William Eaton is not
he author of the extract of a letter above mentioned,
or do I believe that he had any knowledge of it un-
l it appeared in print.

JAMES UNDERHILL.
Bennington, March 21, 1793.

☞ The laws and journals of the laft feffion of af-
embly are fent to the feveral counties, and now ready
or delivery to thofe to whom directed. A few copies
f them are for fale at the printing office, Benning-
on.

WINDSOR, February 23.
On Monday laft, the following melancholly acci-
ent happened in this town.—As two lads, fons of Mr.
Darius Houghton, the oldeft about eight years of age,
nd the youngeft about fix, were under a pole hovel,
here being a large quantity of fnow upon the roof, the
idge pole broke, and the roof, fell in upon the lads,
nd inftantly put a period to the life of the latter—the
ormer was badly wounded, but is in a good way of
ecovery.

Eight Dollars Reward.

RUN-AWAY, on the night of the 13th inft. a
negro fellow named HARRY, about nineteen
or twenty years of age, and about five or fix inches
high, tolerably well made, has been accuftomed principally to houfe work ; he wore when he went away,
a dark grey furtout coat with a green cape, a thickfet
fhort under coat, brown overhalls, white fhirt &c.
s naturally fond of drefs, feemingly fimple in his replies,
and is not very witty : He is fuppofed to have been enticed away by, or gone off with a white man who
has refided in this town for feveral weeks paft, and
calls himfelf James Fofter. Whoever will take up
and return, or fecure faid negro, fo that the fubfcri-
bers may have him again, fhall receive the above reward and reafonable charges.

JANES & DOLE.
Lanfingburgh, Jan. 15, 1793.   43tf.

RUNAWAY SLAVE ADVERTISEMENT, VERMONT GAZETTE (1793)

Overview: Runaway slave advertisements can offer important glimpses into several aspects of an individual slave's life, personality, work, and dressing habits. In this document, Harry's owner described him as a house servant, "naturally fond of dress," and not witty (this could have been Harry's choice to act stupid in order to avoid certain work tasks). The ad also shows the interracial friendship between Harry and James Foster, who had helped him escape.

Source: *Vermont Gazette*, March 22, 1793.

Eight Dollars Reward.

RUN-AWAY, on the night of the 13th inst. a negro fellow named HARRY, about nineteen or twenty years of age, and about five or six inches high [obvious misprint], tolerably well made, has been accustomed principally to house work....[he] is naturally fond of dress, seemingly simple in his replies, and is not very witty. He is supposed to have been enticed away by, or gone off with a white man who has resided in this town for several weeks past, and calls himself James Foster. Whoever will take up and return, or secure said negro, so that the subscribers may have him again, shall receive the above reward and reasonable charges.

JANES & DOLE.
Lansingburgh, [N.Y.] Jan. 15, 1793.

expect soon to have the particulars of this last action. The same news quiets us as to England. Firm and victorious abroad, we want nothing but a good constitution within.

☞ The piece signed, "JUNIUS," addressed to Col. Matthew Lyon—And an "Extract of a letter," published "by desire," in the Lansingburgh Spy, are received, and will appear next week.

List of letters remaining in the Post-Office at Vergennes, April 1, 1793.

JONATHAN GRUN, Hinesburgh, Vermont.

Col. William Harrington, Shelburne, do.

William C. Harrington, attorney at law, Shelburne, do.

Mr. Archibald Brewer, Orwell, do.

Zadock Everest, Addison, do.

Charles Hay, Esq. Ticonderoga, state of Newyork.

ALEXANDER BRUSH,
Deputy Postmaster.

RAN away from the subscriber, a Mulatto Man, by the name of FRANK, about five feet eight inches high, twenty-seven years of age, hath lost two fingers off his left hand, speaks good Dutch and English. Whoever will take up and secure said negro, so that the owner can have him, shall have EIGHT DOLLARS reward, besides all reasonable charges. JOSEPH WALDRON, April 8th, 1793. Coeyman's Patent.

WHEREAS the legislature of the state of Vermont, at their session at Windsor, in October 1791, granted a tax of two pence on each acre of land in Hancock, in the county of Addison, public rights excepted, for the purpose of making and repairing public roads, and building bridges in said town; which tax has been worked out, and the accounts allowed by the county court—these are therefore to notify the proprietors and land owners in said town, who have not paid said tax, that so much of their land will be sold at public vendue, at the house of Joseph Butts, in said Hancock, on the third Tuesday of July next, as will pay said tax and legal cost, unless sooner paid to me the subscriber.——The delinquent proprietors names are as follow, with the sum of thirty shillings due on each right unless otherwise marked

Runaway Slave Advertisement, Vermont Gazette (1793)

Overview: This ad is a typical example of regional owners advertising for the return of their escaped slaves. Frank spoke both Dutch and English, like most slaves in upstate New York/Vermont.

Source: *Vermont Gazette*, April 19, 1793.

RAN *away from the subscriber, a Mulatto Man, by the name of* FRANK, *about five feet eight inches high, twenty-seven years of age, hath lost two fingers off his left hand, speaks good Dutch and English. Whoever will take up and secure said negro, so that the owner can have him, shall have* EIGHT DOLLARS *reward, besides all reasonable charges.*

JOSEPH WALDRON,
April 8th, 1793.   *Coeyman's Patent,* [N.Y.]

ngton, *June* 28th, 1793.

FIFTEEN DOLLARS *Reward.*

RAN *away from the subscriber, the 25th of June instant, a negro man named JAMES, about five feet nine inches high, is midling black, speaks Dutch and English very well, had with him a white linen coat, a homespun sailor's jacket, and overalls, brown linen trowsers, a red and a spotted waistecoat, and a high crowned castor hat. He is about thirty years of age. Whosoever will take up said NEGRO, and return him to his master, shall receive the above reward, by me,*

WALTER VAN VEGHTEN.
Cambridge, Washington county,
June 26th, 1793.

THE subscriber has in the townships of Alburgh, Highgate, and Swanton bounded on Lake Champlain, and in Coventry and Irasburgh, contiguous to Lake Mumphreymagog, all in the county of Chittenden, and state of Vermont, about one hundred thousand acres of Land, that he will lease on reasona-

RUNAWAY SLAVE ADVERTISEMENT,
VERMONT GAZETTE (1793)

Overview: This runaway ad does not tell historians much about James aside from his skin color, age, and ability to speak Dutch and English.

Source: *Vermont Gazette*, June 28, 1793.

FIFTEEN DOLLARS Reward.
RAN away from the subscriber, the 25th of June instant, a negro man named JAMES, about five feet nine inches high, is midling black, speaks Dutch and English very well, had with him a white linen coat, a homespun sailor's jacket, and overalls, brown linen trowsers, a red and a spotted waistcoat, and a high crowned castor hat. He is about thirty years of age. Whosoever will take up said NEGRO, and return him to his master, shall receive the above reward, by me,

WALTER VAN VEGHTEN.
Cambridge, Washington county, [N.Y.]
June 26th, 1793.

Which are now opened at his store in Williamstown, near Williams College, on as reasonable terms as will be met with in New-York or Boston.

☞ *Catalogues given gratis at said store.* 3m t 1 f 3 m

Williamstown, August 11, 1795,

25 Dollars Reward.

RANAWAY from the subscriber, on the 22d instant, a negro man slave, named Joe, about twenty four years old, about five feet ten inches high, had on when he went away, a round black felt hat, a check shirt, a red spotted handkerchief round his neck, a brown coat, a red jacket and tow cloth trowsers or fustian overhalls; the above reward and all reasonable charges will be paid by the subscriber, living in the town of Schaticoke in the county Rensellaer, in the state of Newyork, to any person who will secure the negro slave in any goal in the United States and give notice thereof to the subscriber.

Weynant W. Vandersburgh.

Schaticoke, August 4. 1795. 2t4

HARDWICK.

NOTICE is hereby given that the subscribers will present a petition at the next session of the General Assembly, for a tax of one penny per acre on the township of Hardwick, in the county of Orange, for the purpose of making and repairing highways and building bridges.

PAUL SPOONER,
ALPHA WARNER. 2t4

Hardwick, August 3, 1795.

GREENSBOROUGH.

committed to the ...
therefore to warn the p...
land owners in said Bart...
tax to me the subscriber,
second day of November n...
of their of lands will be
ond day of November, at
the forenoon, of said day
house of Timothy Stanl...
rough.

TIM. STAN...

Windsor, July 20th, 17...

NOTICE is hereby
it may concern, that ...
and James Morse, will
to the general assembl...
mont at their session i...
a tax of one penny a...
of Marshfield and Dev...
eys-gore, so called, i...
ange, for the purpose
pairing roads in said t...

Cabot, July 7, 17...

BOL...

I HEREBY not...
land owners of Bo...
Chittenden, that ...
lature of Verm...
October next, for ...
the acre of the la...
the purpose of m...
bridges.

Bolton, July 20...

50 DOL...

RANAWA...
Cambridg...
the 9th inst. a...
about 5 feet 1...
long favored, ...
feet, he is ab...

Runaway Slave Advertisement, Vermont Gazette (1795)

Overview: This advertisement provides information about Joe's height and age, but nothing about his skin color, work patterns, intelligence, or language ability.

Source: *Vermont Gazette*, August 14, 1795.

25 Dollars Reward.
RANAWAY from the subscriber, on the 22d instant, a negro man slave, named Joe, about twenty four years old, about five feet ten inches high, had on when he went away, a round black felt hat, a check shirt, a red spotted handkerchief round his neck, a brown coat, a red jacket and tow cloth trowsers or sustian overhalls; the above reward and all reasonable charges will be paid by the subscriber, living in the town of Schaticoke in the county of Rensellaer, in the state of Newyork, to any person who will secure the negro slave in any goal [jail] in the United States and give notice thereof to the subscriber.

Weynant W. Vandersburgh.
Schaticoke, [N.Y.] August 4. 1795.

This may certify that the within Named William Strong
did apprehend by a Warrant the within Named Timothy
J. Hodgkiss and brought him before me & Daniel Marsh
Esq. of Hartford to answer to a complaint against him
for the intended Murder of a Negro wench whom
he threw into a well, and the s.d Hodgkiss was
bound to appear before the Supreem court and by
said Strong was committed to the Goal in Woodstock, and
s.d Hodgkiss broke Goal and was not brought
to plead before s.d Supreem court —
Windsor Oct 23.d 1797

attest

John Clark Justice of peace

No. 195 Auditors office Windsor Oct 23.d 1797
The with acct. being examined and allowed
the Treasurer is directed to pay the same to
William Strong or bearer the same being Eight
Dollars & fifty five cents ——
$. 8. 55   Elisha Clark auditor

WARRANT FOR TIMOTHY HODGKISS FOR ATTEMPTED MURDER OF A "NEGRO WENCH" (1797)

Overview: Timothy J. Hodgkiss attempted to murder an unnamed black woman by throwing her into a well. It is significant to note that Hodgkiss had been charged and would have faced justice if he had not escaped from the jail. The document shows that white men could face criminal charges if they committed violence against an African American.

Source: Warrant for Timothy Hodgkiss for Attempted Murder of "Negro Wench," 1797, Volume 11, p. 222. Manuscript Vermont State Papers, 1777-1861 (series SE-118). SE118-00011. Vermont State Archives and Records Administration, Middlesex.

This may certify that the within named William Strong did apprehend by a Warrant the within Named Timothy J. Hodgkiss and brought him before me & Daniel Marsh Esq. of Hartford to answer to a complaint against him for the intended Murder of a Negro Wench whom he threw into a well, and the sd. Hodgkiss was bound to appear before the Supreem court, and by [the] said Strong was committed to the goal [jail] in Woodstock, and sd. Hodgkiss broke goal [jail] and was not brought to plead before sd. Supreem court.—

Windsor, Oct 23d. 1797
John Clark, Justice of [the] Peace

Selectmen versus Jacob [DINAH CASE] (1802)

Overview: The *Dinah* trial is one of the most important sources of information about slavery in early Vermont. In this case, the selectmen of Windsor sued Stephen Jacob, a respected member of local society and Supreme Court assistant judge, for money advanced to take care of Jacob's indigent former slave, Dinah. Jacob's attorney argued that slavery did not exist in Vermont (even though everyone knew Jacob had held Dinah in bondage since 1783, as there was a bill of sale to prove this fact—but the judges did not allow it to be admitted as evidence, see Document 9) and that his client should not be held responsible for the expenses the town incurred for caring for Dinah after Jacob kicked her out of his house. The judges agreed and nonsuited the plaintiffs. Strikingly, the question of Jacob's open and public slaveholding received little attention from the court.

Source: Royall Tyler, ed., *Reports of Cases Argued and Determined in the Supreme Court of Judicature of the State of Vermont*, 2 vols. (New York: I. Riley, 1809, 1810), 2: 192-201.

SELECTMEN of Windsor
against
STEPHEN JACOB, Esquire

THE plaintiffs, as selectmen and overseers of the poor of the town of *Windsor*, declared against the defendant in several counts of general *indebitatus assumpsit*.

First. For 100 dollars, money laid out and expended.

Secondly. For work and labour done. Both stated to be on the 1st day of *January*, 1801.

The plaintiffs in their specification stated, That on 26th of *July*, 1783, the defendant purchased of one *White, Dinah*, a negro slave, whom he then brought into the town of *Windsor*; that she continued to live with and serve him as a slave until some time in the year 1800, when she became infirm, sick, and blind, and in this condition was discarded by the defendant, and became a public charge, and that for the moneys expended by the corporation for medicine and attendance during her sickness, and for her support since, this action is brought.

General issue pleaded, and joinder.

In support of the declaration, the plaintiffs offered to read in evidence to the Jury the bill of sale from *White* to the defendant.

Marsh, counsel for defendant, objected. If this action can be supported, it must be on the principle of the implied contract a master is under to maintain his slave. But we contend that no person can be held in slavery in this State; and the showing of a bill of sale can be no evidence that the unfortunate being supposed to be transferred by it as a human chattel, is a slave; for the contract in the bill of sale is void by our constitution, which, in the first article of the declaration of the rights of the inhabitants of the State of *Vermont*, declares, "That all men are born equally free and independent, and have certain natural, inherent, and inalienable rights, among which are the enjoying and defending life and liberty, acquiring, possessing, and protecting property, and pursuing and obtaining happiness and safety: Therefore no male person born in this country, or brought from over sea,

Judgment in the Matter of the Selectmen of Windsor vs. Stephen Jacob, Volume 2, p. 336. Windsor County Supreme Court, August 1796-August 1806. (PRA-244). PRA-01002. Vermont State Archives and Records Administration, Middlesex.

ought to be holden by law to serve any person as a servant, *slave*, or apprentice, after he arrives to the age of twenty-one years; nor *female* in like manner after she arrives to the age of eighteen years, unless they are bound by their own consent after they arrive to such age, or bound by law for the payment of debts, damages, fines, costs, or the like."

It will not be contended that the *African Dinah* is within the exceptions to this fundamental right.

Hubbard, for the plaintiffs, replied,

That though no person can hold a slave *de jure* by our constitution, yet there may exist among us a slave *de facto*. That if a master will hold an *African* in bondage as a slave, contrary to right, and for a succession of years, during which the slave *de facto* spends the vigour of her life in his service, and in which she may be presumed to have earned for the master sufficient to maintain her in the decrepitude of old age, there is a moral obligation upon the master to support her when incapable of labour; and the law of common justice, upon which all equitable actions are founded, will imply a promise in him to respond [refund?] any necessary expenses incurred by others for her support.

That it would operate extremely hard upon corporations, who possessed no power to loose the shackles of slavery while the slave continued in health, to be made a common infirmary for them when sick and useless.

That the position, "that slavery cannot exist in this State," must be taken *cum grano salis*; for in case a slave-holder should pass through our territory attended by his slave, the constitution of the *United States* protects the master's tenure in the slave, in case the slave should abscond. "No person held to service or labour in one State under the laws thereof, escaping into another, shall, in consequence of any law, or regulation therein, be discharged from such service or labour, but shall be delivered up on the claim of the party to whom such service or labour may be due;" and by the act of the *United States* "respecting fugitives from justice, and persons escaping from the service of their masters," passed during the second session of the second Congress, the magistrates of this State are holden to aid in the arrest of fugitive slaves; and if they find, on examination, that the fugitive is a slave under the laws of the place from which he fled, they must certify the slavery; and the master or his agent may remove the fugitive as *such*, from this State, and annexing a penalty against all who may impede the slave-holder in seizing his property or rescuing the slave after he has been arrested. The bill of sale in ordinary cases must be admitted by the magistrates to substantiate the slave-holder's right. The principle upon which such bill is founded cannot be drawn into question, for that had been already settled by the article of the *United States* constitution cited. If, therefore, the bill of sale cannot be exhibited in evidence in this case, because it is void by our State constitution, it cannot be shown in any case; and this would avoid the constitution and laws of the *United States*; and, as if to meet the present case, the sixth article of the constitution of the *United States* declares that this constitution, and the laws of the *United States* which shall be made in pursuance thereof, &c. shall be the supreme law of the land, and the Judges in every State shall be bound thereby, any thing in the *constitution* and laws of any State to the contrary notwithstanding.

Marsh, contra. A distinction is attempted to be made between a slave holden *de jure* and a slave *de facto*; and it is urged, that in the latter case there exists a moral obligation in the master of such slave, who has received the benefit of her services, to bear the burthen of her infirmities. There is indeed a moral obligation upon all to be charitable, and to conduct conformably to the principles of natural justice, but we consider that such principles do not operate for, but against the plaintiffs. We beg liberty to state the facts, which, at the same time they do away an illiberal charge made against our client in the specification, will show, that no implied promise in the defendant can be raised in equity to respond [refund?] moneys expended by the plaintiffs in support of the slave *de facto*.

Some time in the year 1783, the defendant brought the woman *Dinah* into this State. She continued in his family several years; and there can be but little doubt, from the excellent character and disposition of her master, she would have so continued until this time in sickness and in health; but several of the inhabitants of *Windsor*, represented in their corporate capacity by the present plaintiffs, discovering that she was an excellent servant, and wishing to profit themselves of her labours, inveigled her from her master's family and service by the syren songs of *liberty and equality*, which have too often turned wiser heads. She spent the vigour of her life with these people, and wasted her strength in their service; and now she is blind, paralytic, and incapable of labour, they aim by this suit to compel the defendant *solely* to maintain her; for as a member of the corporation, on the event of the failure of this suit, he must bear his proportion of the burthen.

When she was enticed from the defendant's service, he did not attempt by legal aid to reclaim her. As an inhabitant of the State, in obedience to the constitution, he considered that he could not hold her as a slave. Is it equitable then, that when the sovereign power had dissolved the tenure by which he held her services, and when he had been deprived of her labours by the enticement of others, that by the same power, and *virtually* at the suit

of the same people who enticed her from his service, and who have profited
by her labours when in vigor and health, he should now be compelled to
maintain her in the decrepitancy of old age.

It is said, that it is extremely hard for a corporation, who possessed
no power to remove the slave *de facto* from her master whilst in health, to
be compelled to support her when sick or infirm.

The corporation of *Windsor* should have availed itself of the provision of the act in this as in all other like cases, by warning her to depart the
town, which is the only mode pointed out in the statutes to avert from a
town corporation the expense of maintaining a pauper.

It is said, that by the operation of the constitution and laws of the
United States, slavery may be said to exist in this State in a qualified sense. We
are not disposed to investigate this position. It is certainly more curious than
important in its application to the case in question. In this case the right of
a claimant to a fugitive slave is not in issue. The simple point is, is the defendant obligated to refund moneys advanced by others for medicine and attendance, and in support of a woman who had formerly been in his service? We
contend that it cannot be upon any other principle than that she is his slave;
which cannot be admitted under our constitution of government.

TYLER, Assistant Judge. The plaintiffs, as selectmen, and overseers
of the poor of the town of *Windsor*, have declared in two general counts, and
have displayed their cause of action in their specification, and rest it upon
the implied liability the defendant is under to defray the expenses incurred
by the sickness, and for the support of a blind aged person, who they allege
is the defendant's slave, purchased by a regular bill of sale. In support of the
declaration, this bill of sale is offered, and an exception is taken to its being
read as evidence to the Jury. The question must turn upon the validity or
operative force of this instrument *within this State*. If the bill of sale could
by our constitution operate to bind the woman in slavery when brought by
the defendant to inhabit within this State, then it ought to be admitted in
evidence; and the law will raise a liability in the slave-holder to maintain
her through all the vicissitudes of life; but if otherwise it is void.

Our State constitution is express, no inhabitant of the State can
hold a slave; and though the bill of slave may be binding by the *lex loci* of
another State or dominion, yet when the master becomes an inhabitant of
this State, his bill of sale ceases to operate here.

With respect to what has been observed upon the constitution and
laws of the Union, I will observe, that whoever views attentively the constitution of the *United States*, while he admires the wisdom which framed

it, will perceive, that in order to unite the interests of a numerous people
inhabiting a broad extent of territory, and possessing from education and
habits, different modes of thinking upon important subjects, it was necessary to make numerous provisions in favour of local prejudices, and so to
construct the constitution, and so to enact the laws made under it, that
the rights or the supposed rights of all should be secured throughout the
whole national domain. In compliance with the spirit of this constitution,
upon our admission to the Federal Union, the statute laws of this State were
revised, and a penal act, which was supposed to militate against the third
member of 2d section of the 4th article of the constitution of the *United
States*, was repealed; and if cases shall happen in which our local sentiments
and feelings may be violated, yet I trust the good people of *Vermont* will on
all such occasions submit with cheerfulness to the national constitution
and laws, which, if we may in some particular wish more congenial to our
modes of thinking, yet we must be sensible are productive of numerous
and rich blessings to us as individuals, and to the State as an integral of the
Union.

The question under consideration is not affected by the constitution or laws of the *United States*. It depends solely upon the construction of
our own State constitution, as operative upon the inhabitants of the State;
which, as it does not admit of the idea of slavery in any of its inhabitants,
the contract which considers a person inhabiting the State territory as such,
must be void. I am therefore against admitting the bill of sale in evidence.

Chief Judge. I concur fully in opinion with the Assistant Judge. I
shall always respect the constitution and laws of the Union; and though it
may sometimes be a reluctant, yet I shall always render a prompt obedience
to them, fully sensible, that while I reverence a constitution and laws which
favour the opinions and prejudices of the citizens of other sections of the
Union, the same constitution and laws contain also provisions which favour
our peculiar opinions and prejudices, and which may possibly be equally
irreconcilable with the sentiments of the inhabitants of other States, as the
very idea of slavery is to us. But when the question of slavery involves solely
the interests of the inhabitants of this State, I shall cheerfully carry into effect the enlightened principles of our State constitution.

The bill of sale cannot be read in evidence to the Jury.

Plaintiffs nonsuited.

Jonathan Hatch Hubbard and *Amasa Paine*, for plaintiffs.
Charles Marsh and *Jacob Smith*, for defendant.

REJECTION OF MASSACHUSETTS'S PROPOSAL TO ALTER THE FEDERAL 3/5 RATIO (1804)

Overview: Massachusetts wanted to overturn the 3/5 ratio that gave the South increased representation in the federal House of Representatives for its slave population. (This advantage had been guaranteed to the South in the United States Constitution). The legislators in Massachusetts thought that Vermont would be a natural ally in attempting to restructure the representation of the House of Representatives. But Vermont rejected Massachusetts because the 3/5 ratio had been "the result of a spirit of compromise" at the 1787 Constitutional Convention and the South saw representation for slaves as a "sacred" right. Vermont did not want to upset the slaveholding and slave-trading states by challenging this "sacred right."

Source: E. P. Walton, ed., *Records of the Governor and Council of the State of Vermont*, 8 vols. (Montpelier, Vt.: Steam Press of J. & J. M. Poland, 1873-1880), 5: 414-15; *Journals of the General Assembly of the State of Vermont, 1804* (Bennington, Vt.: Haswell & Smead, 1805), 266-68.

[November 2, 1804]

The amendment proposed, as we conceive, would materially affect a part of the federal constitution which was in fact the result of a spirit of compromise, and which guarantees to some of the States in the Union, a right, which to them is sacred; a right, in consideration of which, mutual benefits are secured to us. For although the duties arising from imports are sufficient to meet the exigencies of government, while we enjoy the calm sunshine of peace; yet, should the United States at any time be involved in war, (which is no uncommon fate of nations,) very important would be the power, and very necessary the use of direct taxation. And in such an event, we should highly appreciate the mode of apportioning the expences among the several States, established by our present Constitution.

Again, we apprehend that the amendment proposed would have a tendency to destroy, rather than confirm, that union among the several States, so essential to our national prosperity.

quested to transmit to each of the said Senators an attested copy of this Resolution.

And it is hereby further Resolved, That His Excellency the Governor be requested to inform the Chief Magistrates of the several States of the doings of the Legislature of this Commonwealth, and request them to adopt the same measures.

Sent up for concurrence.   H. G. OTIS, *Speaker.*

IN SENATE, June 20, 1804.   Read and concurred.

D. COBB, *President.*

A true Copy,   Attest,   JOHN AVERY, *Secretary.*

Oct. 18 1804, the foregoing resolutions were considered by the Assembly in committee of the whole, and the report was adverse. After debate on the report in the House, the question of acceptance was postponed to the 25th, when, "after a lengthy discussion of the subject," the report was accepted, yeas 106 to nays 76. In the Presidential election of 1800, Mr. Jefferson received 73 votes, 53 of which were from the slave states; and John Adams received 65 votes, 53 of which were from the free states: so Mr. Jefferson's votes were mainly from the slave, and those of Mr. Adams from the free states. This fact was adverted to in the preamble to the resolution adopted by Massachusetts, which was then a Federal State. That both the Jeffersonians and the Federalists in the legislature treated this as a party question, is evident from the yeas and nays. Among those who favored the adverse report of the committee were the following prominent Jeffersonians: William C. Bradley, Ezra Butler, James Fisk, Titus Hutchinson, Aaron Leland, Henry Olin, Mark Richards, Charles Rich, and Samuel Shaw, all of whom but two became Congressmen; while among the nays were prominent Federalists, to wit, Jedediah P. Buckingham, Daniel Chipman, Arad Hunt, Wm. C. Harrington, Asa Lyon, and Solomon Wright. On the next day, James Fisk, Titus Hutchinson, and Charles Rich were appointed to draft a message or reply to Governor Tichenor on the subject, and on the second of November they reported as follows:

Sir,—The resolutions transmitted by the Governor of Massachusetts, and which accompanied your message of October 13th, 1804, have received from this House that consideration which the importance of the subject requires.

We do not consider the provisions of the present constitution so unequal as supposed by said resolutions; nor do we consider those provisions to have been rendered more injurious by any political changes introduced during the present administration.

The amendment proposed, as we conceive, would materially affect a part of the federal constitution which was in fact the result of a spirit of compromise, and which guarantees to some of the States in the Union, a right, which to them is sacred; a right, in consideration of which, mutual benefits are secured to us. For although the duties arising from imports are sufficient to meet the exigencies of government, while we enjoy the calm sunshine of peace; yet, should the United States at any time be involved in war, (which is no uncommon fate of nations,) very important would be the power, and very necessary the use of direct taxation. And in such an event, we should highly appreciate the mode was read, and referred to the firſt turnpike committee.

The petition of William Barton, referred from the laſt ſeſſion of the legiſlature, was called up, and referred to a committee of five, to join a committee from the coucil.

Members choſen, Meſſrs. Hunt, Pearl, Shaw, Bullock and Hurd.

A bill entitled an act relating to boarding ſtate's priſoners the year paſt, was taken up and amended, read the ſecond time, paſſed, ordered to be engroſſed and ſent to the governor and council for their reviſion and concurrence, or propoſals of amendment.

The petition of William Wallace was read and referred to the committee of inſolvency and ſuſpenſion.

The committee to whom was committed the bill entitled an act to enable the ſelect men of the ſeveral towns in this ſtate to lay out private roads through the ſame where neceſſary, and to ſecure the ſame by gates as circumſtance may require,—made report, that, in their opinion the bill ought to paſs and become a law of this ſtate.

Which report was accepted, and the bill was read and ordered to lie for a ſecond reading tomorrow afternoon.

The order of the day was called for, on the conſideration of the reſolutions communicated from the governors of Kentucky and North-Carolina.

The reſolution communicated from the governor of North-Carolina was taken up and read,——When,

Mr. Morris, on motion of leave, introduced the following reſolutions.

—

In General Assembly, October 17, 1805.

Reſolved, That our ſenators in the congreſs of the United States be inſtructed, and our repreſentatives requeſted, to take all legal and neceſſary ſteps, to uſe their utmoſt exertions, as ſoon as the ſame is practicable, to obtain an amendment to the Federal Conſtitution, ſo as to authoriſe and empower the congreſs of the United States to paſs a law, whenever they may deem it expedient, to prevent the further importation of ſlaves, or people of colour, from any of the Weſt India iſlands, from the coaſt of Africa or elſewhere, into the United States or any part thereof.

Reſolved, That the governor be, and he is hereby requeſted to tranſmit copies of the foregoing reſolution, to our ſenators and repreſentatives in congreſs ; alſo to the executives of all the different ſtates in the Union, with a requeſt that the ſame may be laid before their reſpective legiſlatures, for their concurrence and adoption.

Which reſolutions were read and adopted, and ordered to be ſent to the governor and council for concurrence.

The reſolution communicated from the governor of Kentucky was read, and on motion,

STATEMENT OF THE VERMONT ASSEMBLY ABOUT SLAVERY AND THE SLAVE TRADE (1805)

Overview: The Vermont Assembly strongly opposed the slave trade and wanted the traffic to be banned as soon as possible (1808 was the earliest date according to the United States Constitution). However, the selection below indicates that the Vermont Assembly opposed not only the further importation of slaves, but also the immigration of people of color to the United States.

Source: *Journals of the General Assembly of the State of Vermont, 1805* (Windsor, Vt.: Alden Spooner, 1806), 54.

In General Assembly, *October* 17, 1805.

Resolved, That our senators in the congress of the United States be instructed, and our representatives requested, to take all legal and necessary steps, to use their utmost exertions, as soon as the same is practicable, to obtain an amendment to the Federal Constitution, so as to authorize and empower the congress of the United States to pass a law, whenever they may deem it expedient, to prevent the further importation of slaves, or people of colour, from any of the West India islands, from the coast of Africa or elsewhere, into the United States or any part thereof.

Middlebury, Friday, October 31st 1806 —

compact form, and of noticing the existing variations, between those acts, and the revised laws, published by the authority of the Legislature, in the year 1798. —

Read, adopted and Mess[rs] Bradley, Aiken and Whitney were appointed a Committee on the part of the house

A.H. M. Port Clk[s]

and the same being read,

Ordered. That M[r] Galusha join the Committee, on the above resolution—

The following resolution was received from the house: —

"In General Assembly Oct 30, 1806. — Whereas there have been a number of instances of Negro persons, who were minors, having been transported by evil minded persons, from this to the other States and province of Canada, where slavery is established by law, and there disposed of as slaves † which practice is contrary to the Genius and principles of the good people and Government of this state, and, Therefore, the evil of which pernicious practices to prevent, — Resolved there be a committee of five members to join from Council, to take under consideration the propriety of passing a law, for remedying the evils abovementioned, and report to this house, by bill or otherwise — Read, adopted, and Mess[rs]. Hendee, Williams, E. Robinson, Hinman and Houm were appointed a Committee on the part of the house — Attest M. Port Clk" —

and the same being read,

Ordered. That M[r] Shepardson join the above Committee from the house—

The following bills, passed in the house of Representatives, were sent up for revision and concurrence, or proposals of amendment—

"An act, directing the Treasurer of this State, to credit the town of Stockbridge, the sum therein mentioned,"

"An act, laying a Tax of three cents per acre, on all the lands within the original grant of the township of New Huntington, Buels and Avery's Gore,"

"An act, laying a tax of three cents, per acre on the town of Hopkinsie,"

"An act, directing the Treasurer of this State, to credit the Town of Wells, the sum therein mentioned," and,

"An act, assessing a Tax of one cent on the dollar, on the list of the present year," and the same being severally read and considered,

Resolved. To concur with the house, in passing them respectively, into laws

Adjourned to 2 o'clock P.M.

PREVENTION OF KIDNAPPING ACT (1806)

Overview: The Prevention of Kidnapping Act (1806) admitted that black people were still being enslaved and sold out of the state despite the 1777 provision and the 1786 law. The Kidnapping Act threatened to punish those guilty of trafficking black people with 39 lashes and up to 7 years in prison.

Source: Journal of the Council of the State of Vermont, October 31, 1806, volume 5, p. 284. *Journal of the Council of Safety and Journals of the Governor and Council* (Executive Council), 1777-1835 (Series A-010). A010-00006. Vermont State Archives and Records Administration, Middlesex. See also E. P. Walton, ed., *Records of the Governor and Council of the State of Vermont*, 8 vols. (Montpelier, Vt.: Steam Press of J. & J. M. Poland, 1873-1880), 5: 131; *Acts and Laws, Passed by the Legislature of the State of Vermont, 1806* (Bennington, Vt.: Anthony Haswell, 1806), 151-52.

In General Assembly Oct 30, 1806.—Whereas there have been a number of instances of Negro persons, who were minors, having been transported by evil minded persons from this to the other States and [the] province of Canada, where slavery is established by law, and there disposed of as slaves, which practice is contrary to the Genius and principles of the good people and Government of this state, and, Therefore, the evil of which pernicious practices to prevent, —Resolved there be a Committee of five members to join from Council, to take under consideration the propriety of passing a law, for remedying the evils abovementioned, and report to this house, by bill or otherwise.

An Act to prevent kidnapping

It is hereby enacted by the General Assembly of the State of Vermont, That if any person or persons, shall directly, or indirectly, be guilty of carrying, removing, or aiding and assisting, in transporting any person, or persons, who are, or shall be residents in this state, into any other state, province or government, and there dispose of the same into servitude, for longer term of time, or in a different manner than he, she or they could have a right, by law to do within this state, and shall be thereof convicted before the supreme court, shall be publicly whipped, on his naked back, not exceeding thirty nine stripes, or pay a fine, not exceeding one thousand dollars, and be confined to hard labor, or imprisonment, not exceeding seven years; any part, or the whole of the aforesaid punishment to be inflicted, or penalty to be imposed, at the discretion of said court; and shall be further liable to make good all damages, to the person thus carried away, removed, or disposed of.

Passed November 8th, 1806.

1810 United States Census, Town Returns (1810)

Overview: Surprisingly, two Vermonters are listed as owning slaves in the 1810 census. Both men, Joseph Woodward and Epaphras Jones, resided in Addison County (in the towns of Leicester and Salisbury, respectively). Please note the mark in the far right hand column, where slaves were tabulated.

Source: Population Schedules, 3rd Census, 1810, Vermont, NARA #M252, Reel 65, #2, Special Collections, Bailey/Howe Library, University of Vermont, Burlington.

Addison County

Leicester: Joseph Woodward   1 slave

Salisbury: Epaphras Jones   1 slave

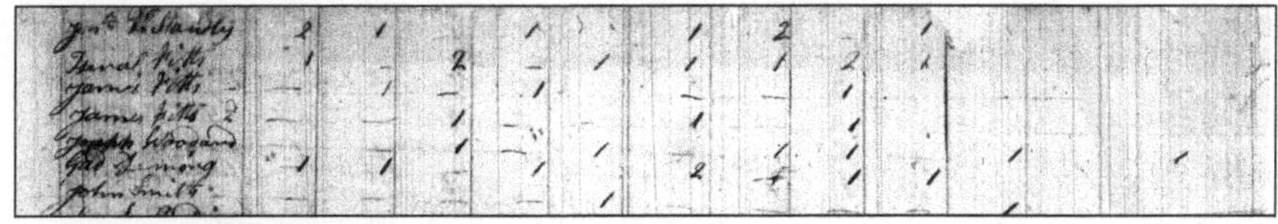

Document Sources

SCUVM Special Collections, Bailey/Howe Library, University of Vermont, Burlington.

VSARA Vermont State Archives and Records Administration, Middlesex.

Document 1: Bill of Sale, John Barrett purchased Rose, July 5, 1770. Topsham John Barrett Papers, Town Clerk's Office, Topsham, Vermont. On deposit at SCUVM.

Document 2: Abolition of Adult Slavery, July 2, 1777. Vermont Constitution, Chapter 1, "A Declaration of the Rights of the Inhabitants of the State of Vermont," Vermont Constitution 1777 (A-014). MAP-A28.4. VSARA.

Document 3: Manumission of Dinah Mattis and her daughter, November 28, 1777. Abby M. Hemenway, ed., *The Vermont Historical Gazetteer*, Volume 2 (Burlington, Vt.: Miss A. M. Hemenway, 1871), p. 580.

Document 4: Formation of a Committee to Prepare a Bill Regarding the Freedom of Slaves, October 24, 1778, Volume 1, p. 65. Joint Assembly Journals, 1778-1965. (A-113) A113-00001. VSARA.

Document 5: An Account of Leonard Spaulding [Commissioner of Sequestration], Regarding Tory estate of Timothy Lovel and a bill of sale for Pomp Brake, June 22, 1778, Volume 37, p. 26. Manuscript Vermont State Papers, 1777-1861 (series SE-118). SE118-00037. VSARA.

Document 6: Story of Slaveholding Bennington Minister, 1780. Abby M. Hemenway, ed., *The Vermont Historical Gazetteer*, Volume 1 (Burlington, Vt.: Miss A. M. Hemenway, 1867), p. 163.

Document 7: John Armstrong, Probate Record, April–May 1782. Probate Records, Bennington Probate Division, Vermont Superior Court, Bennington.

Document 8: Bill of Sale, John Barrett purchased Rose from Samuel Andrew, April 3, 1783. Topsham John Barrett Papers, Town Clerk's Office, Topsham, Vermont. On deposit at SCUVM.

Document 9: Bill of Sale, Stephen Jacob purchased Dinah from Jotham White, 1783/1801. Jotham White, typed copy of Bill of Sale of a Negro Woman Slave, Dinah, executed to Stephen Jacob, July 26, 1783, with note appended July 20, 1801, XMS 326 W582. Vermont Historical Society, Barre.

Document 10: Levi Allen to Jacob Lansingh, December 3, 1784. Collection of the Fort Ticonderoga Museum, Ticonderoga, New York.

Document 11: "An Act to Prevent the Sale and Transportation of Negroes & Molattos out of this State," October 30, 1786, Volume 1, p. 555. Manuscript Laws of Vermont, circa 1778-1968, (A-112). A112-00001. VSARA.

Document 12: Runaway Slave Advertisement, *Vermont Gazette*, July 3, 1786.

Document 13: Bennington Friendly Society, Minute Book, April 10, 1789, p. 57. SCUVM.

Document 14: Bill of Sale, Oliver Hastings purchased Anthony from Jotham White (1790). Charles H. Hubbard and Justus Dartt, *History of the Town of Springfield, Vermont* (Boston: George H. Walker & Co., 1895), p. 489.

Document 15: Federal Census for Vermont (1791). *Heads of Families at the First Census of the United States Taken in the Year 1790, Vermont* (Washington, D.C.: Government Printing Office, 1907).

Document 16: Selectmen of Rutland Petition for Compensation for Care Given by Town to a Sick Negro, a Foreigner, 1791, Volume 18, p. 234. Manuscript Vermont State Papers, 1777-1861 (series SE-118). SE118-00018. VSARA.

Document 17: "An Act Respecting Negr[oes] & Molattoes," January 24, 1791, Volume 3, p. 80. Manuscript Vermont State Papers 1777-1861 (series SE-118). SE118-00003. VSARA.

Document 18: Runaway Slave Advertisement, *Vermont Gazette*, July 25, 1791.

Document 19: Runaway Slave Advertisement, *Vermont Gazette*, July 27, 1792.

Document 20: Runaway Slave Advertisement, *Vermont Gazette*, October 19, 1792.

Document 21: "An Act for Regulating and Governing the Militia of the State of Vermont and for Repealing All Laws Heretofore Passed for the Purpose," October 29, 1793, Volume 3, p. 49. Manuscript Laws of Vermont, circa 1778-1968. (A-112). A112-00003. VSARA.

Document 22: Runaway Slave Advertisement, *Vermont Gazette*, March 22, 1793.

Document 23: Runaway Slave Advertisement, *Vermont Gazette*, April 19, 1793.

Document 24: Runaway Slave Advertisement, *Vermont Gazette*, June 28, 1793.

Document 25: Runaway Slave Advertisement, *Vermont Gazette*, August 14, 1795.

Document 26: Warrant for Timothy Hodgkiss for Attempted Murder of "Negro Wench," October 23, 1797, Volume 11, p. 222. Manuscript Vermont State Papers, 1777-1861 (series SE-118). SE118-00011. VSARA.

Document 27: Royall Tyler, ed., *Reports of Cases Argued and Determined in the Supreme Court of Judicature of the State of Vermont*, 2 vols. (New York: I. Riley, 1809, 1810), 2: 192-201.

Document 28: Rejection of Massachusetts's Proposal to Alter the Federal 3/5 Ratio, October 18, 1804. E. P. Walton, ed., *Records of the Governor and Council of the State of Vermont*, 8 volumes (Montpelier, Vt.: Steam Press of J. & J. M. Poland, 1873-1880), 5: 414-15.

Document 29: Statement of the Vermont Assembly about Slavery and the Slave Trade, October 17, 1805. *Journals of the General Assembly of the State of Vermont, 1805* (Windsor, Vt.: Alden Spooner, 1806), p. 54.

Document 30: "An Act to Prevent Kidnapping" (1806). Journal of the Council of the State of Vermont, October 31, 1806, Volume 5, p. 284. *Journal of the Council of Safety and Journals of the Governor and Council (Executive Council), 1777-1835* (Series A-010). A010-00006. VSARA.

Document 31: 1810 United States Census, Town Returns (1810). Population Schedules, 3rd Census, 1810, Vermont, NARA #M252, Reel 65, #2. SCUVM.

Bibliography

126   MANUSCRIPT SOURCES

Vermont State Archives and Records Administration, Middlesex

Document 2: Vermont Constitution, Chapter 1, "A Declaration of the Rights of the Inhabitants of the State of Vermont," Vermont Constitution 1777 (A-014). MAP-A28.4.

Document 4: Formation of a Committee to Prepare a Bill Regarding the Freedom of Slaves, October 24, 1778, Volume 1, p. 65. Joint Assembly Journals, 1778-1965. (A-113) A113-00001.

Document 5: An Account of Leonard Spaulding [Commissioner of Sequestration], Regarding Tory estate of Timothy Lovel and a bill of sale for Pomp Brake, Volume 37, p. 26. Manuscript Vermont State Papers, 1777-1861 (series SE-118). SE118-00037.

Document 11: "An Act to Prevent the Sale and Transportation of Negroes & Molattos out of this State," October 30, 1786, Volume 1, p. 555. Manuscript Laws of Vermont, circa 1778-1968, (A-112). A112-00001.

Document 16: Selectmen of Rutland Petition for Compensation for Care Given by Town to a Sick Negro, a Foreigner, 1791, Volume 18, p. 234. Manuscript Vermont State Papers, 1777-1861 (series SE-118). SE118-00018.

Document 17: "An Act Respecting Negr[oes] & Molattoes," January 24, 1791, Volume 3, p. 80. Manuscript Vermont State Papers 1777-1861 (series SE-118). SE118-00003.

Document 21: "An Act for Regulating and Governing the Militia of the State of Vermont and for Repealing All Laws Heretofore Passed for the Purpose," October 29, 1793, Volume 3, p. 49. Manuscript Laws of Vermont, circa 1778-1968. (A-112). A112-00003.

Document 26: Warrant for Timothy Hodgkiss for Attempted Murder of "Negro Wench," 1797, Volume 11, p. 222. Manuscript Vermont State Papers, 1777-1861 (series SE-118). SE118-00011.

Document 27: Judgment in the Matter of the Selectmen of Windsor vs. Stephen Jacob, Volume 2, p. 336. Windsor County Supreme Court, August 1796-August 1806. (PRA-244). PRA-01002. This is the summary judgment, as shown on p. 109. The report of the proceedings comes from a printed source.

Document 30: Journal of the Council of the State of Vermont, October 31, 1806, volume 5, p. 284. *Journal of the Council of Safety and Journals of the Governor and Council (Executive Council), 1777-1835 (Series A-010).* A010-00006.

Other Archives

Documents 1, 8: Topsham John Barrett Papers, Town Clerk's Office, Topsham, Vermont. On deposit at Special Collections, Bailey/Howe Library, University of Vermont, Burlington.

Document 7: Probate Records, Bennington Probate Division, Vermont Superior Court, Bennington.

Document 10: Levi Allen to Jacob Lansingh, December 3, 1784. Collection of the Fort Ticonderoga Museum, Ticonderoga, New York.

Document 13: Bennington Friendly Society, Minute Book, Special Collections, Bailey/Howe Library, University of Vermont, Burlington.

Vermont Manuscript Files, Special Collections, Bailey/Howe Library, University of Vermont, Burlington.

GOVERNMENT DOCUMENTS

State Papers of Vermont

Volume 3, part 1: Walter H. Crockett, ed. *Journals and Proceedings of the General Assembly of the State of Vermont.* Bellows Falls: P. H. Gobie Press, 1924.

Volume 3, part 4: Walter H. Crockett, ed. *Journals and Proceedings of the State of Vermont.* Bellows Falls: The Wyndham Press, 1929.

Volume 6: *Sequestration, Confiscation, Sale of Estates.* Mary G. Nye, ed. Montpelier, Vt.: Secretary of State, 1941.

Volume 9: *General Petitions, 1788-1792.* Edward A. Hoyt, ed. Montpelier, Vt.: Howard E. Armstrong, Secretary of State, 1955.

Volume 14: *Laws of Vermont.* John A. Williams, ed. Montpelier, Vt.: Secretary of State, 1966.

Newspapers

Bennington, *Vermont Gazette*, 1786-1795

Books and Articles (Primary and Secondary)

Aichele, Gary J. "Making the Vermont Constitution: 1777-1824." *Vermont History* 57 (Summer 1988): 166-90.

Allen, Ethan. *A Vindication of the Opposition of the Inhabitants of Vermont to the Government of New-York and of their right to form into an independent state: humbly submitted to the consideration of the impartial world*. Dresden: Alden Spooner, 1779.

Avery, David. *A Narrative of the Rise and Progress of the Difficulties which have issued in Separation between the Minister and People of Bennington, 1783*. Bennington, Vt.: Haswell and Russell, 1783.

Bailyn, Bernard. *The Ideological Origins of the American Revolution*. 1967; second edition, Cambridge, Mass.: Harvard University Press, 1992.

Baker, Mary E. *Folklore of Springfield*. Springfield, Vt., 1922.

Bandel, Betty. "'Satisfaction Brought It Back.'" *Vermont History News* 30 (Nov.-Dec. 1979): 91-92.

Barney, Keith R. *The History of Springfield, Vermont, 1885-1961, With an Introductory Chapter to 1885*. Springfield, Vt.: William L. Bryant Foundation, 1972.

Bassett, T. D. Seymour. *The Gods of the Hills: Piety and Society in Nineteenth-Century Vermont*. Barre: Vermont Historical Society, 2000.

Beach, Allen P. *The Basin Harbor Story*. Vergennes, Vt.: Basin Harbor Club, 1963.

Benes, Peter, ed. *Slavery/Antislavery in New England—The Dublin Seminar for New England Folklife Annual Proceedings, 2003*. Boston: Boston University, 2005.

Berlin, Ira. *Many Thousands Gone: The First Two Centuries of Slavery in North America*. Cambridge, Mass.: Harvard University Press, 1998.

———— and Leslie M. Harris, eds. *Slavery in New York*. New York: The New Press, 2005.

Bly, Antonio T., ed. *Escaping Bondage: A Documentary History of Runaway Slaves in Eighteenth-Century New England, 1700-1789*. Lanham, Md.: Lexington Books, 2012.

Bonaventura, Allegra di. *For Adam's Sake: A Family Saga in Colonial New England*. New York: W. W. Norton [Liverright], 2013.

Bradley, Patricia. *Slavery, Propaganda, and the American Revolution.* Jackson: University Press of Mississippi, 1998.

Burin, Eric. *Slavery and the Peculiar Solution: A History of the American Colonization Society.* Gainesville: University Press of Florida, 2005.

Bushnell, Mark. *It Happened in Vermont.* Guilford, Conn.: Globe Pequot Press, 2009.

Chipman, Daniel. *A Memoir of Thomas Chittenden, the First Governor of Vermont; with a history of the constitution during his administration.* Middlebury, Vt.: Published by the Author, 1849.

Cogliano, Francis D. *Revolutionary America: A Political History, 1763-1815.* London: Routledge, 2000.

Conlin, Katherine E. "Dinah and the Slave Question in Vermont." *Vermont Quarterly* 21 (October 1953): 289-91.

Davis, David Brion. *Inhuman Bondage: The Rise and Fall of Slavery in the New World.* New York: Oxford University Press, 2006.

———. *The Problem of Slavery in the Age of Revolution, 1770-1823.* 1975; reprint, New York: Oxford University Press, 1999.

Desrochers, Robert E. "Slave-For-Sale Advertisements and Slavery in Massachusetts, 1704-1781." *William and Mary Quarterly* 59 (July 2002): 623-64.

Deutsch, Sarah. "The Elusive Guineamen: Newport Slavers, 1735-1774." *New England Quarterly* 55 (1982): 229-53.

Donoghue, John. "'Out of the Land of Bondage': The English Revolution and the Atlantic Origins of Abolition." *American Historical Review* 115 (October 2010): 943-74.

Dorsey, Peter A. *Common Bondage: Slavery as Metaphor in Revolutionary America.* Knoxville: University of Tennessee Press, 2009.

Elgersman, Maureen G. *Unyielding Spirits: Black Women and Slavery in Early Canada and Jamaica.* New York: Garland Publishing, 1999.

Faherty, Duncan. "'It Happened Here': Slavery on the Hudson." *American Quarterly* 58 (2006): 455-66.

Farrow, Anne, Joel Lang, and Jennifer Frank. *Complicity: How the North Promoted, Prolonged, and Profited From Slavery.* New York: Ballantine, 2006.

Finkelman, Paul. *Slavery and the Founders: Race and Liberty in the Age of Jefferson.* 1996. Second edition, Armonk: M. E. Sharpe, 2001.

Fitts, Robert K. *Inventing New England's Slave Paradise: Master/Slave Relations in Eighteenth-Century Narragansett, Rhode Island.* New York: Garland, 1998.

Foote, Thelma W. *Black and White Manhattan: The History of Racial Formation in Colonial New York City.* New York: Oxford University Press, 2004.

Frederickson, George. *Racism: A Short History.* Princeton, N.J.: Princeton University Press, 2002.

Furstenberg, François. "Beyond Freedom and Slavery: Autonomy, Virtue, and Resistance in Early American Political Discourse." *Journal of American History* 89 (March 2003): 1295-1330.

Gerzina, Gretchen H. *Mr. and Mrs. Prince: How an Extraordinary Eighteenth-Century Family Moved Out of Slavery and into Legend.* New York: Amistad, 2008.

Graffagnino, J. Kevin. "Vermont Attitudes Toward Slavery: The Need For A Closer Look." *Vermont History* 61 (Winter 1977): 31-34.

Greene, Jack P. "'Slavery or Independence': Some Reflections on the Relationship Among Liberty, Black Bondage, and Equality in Revolutionary South Carolina." *South Carolina Historical Magazine* 80 (July 1979): 193-214.

Greene, Lorenzo J. *The Negro in Colonial New England.* 1942; reprint, New York: Atheneum, 1968.

Guyette, Elise A. *Discovering Black Vermont: African American Farmers in Hinesburgh, 1790-1870.* Lebanon, N.H.: University of Vermont Press, published by the University Press of New England, 2010.

———. "The Working Lives of African Vermonters in Census and Literature." *Vermont History* 61 (Spring 1993): 69-84.

Hall, Benjamin H. *History of Eastern Vermont: From its Earliest Settlement to the Close of the Eighteenth Century.* New York: D. Appleton & Co., 1858.

Hammond, John C. *Slavery, Freedom, and Expansion in the Early American West.* Charlottesville: University of Virginia Press, 2007.

Harris, Leslie M. *In the Shadow of Slavery: African Americans in New York City, 1626-1863.* Chicago: University of Chicago Press, 2003.

Heads of Families at the First Census of the United States Taken in the Year 1790, Vermont. Washington, D.C.: Government Printing Office, 1907.

Heads of Families at the Second Census of the United States Taken in the Year 1800, Vermont. Montpelier: Vermont Historical Society, 1938.

Hemenway, Abby M., editor. *The Vermont Historical Gazetteer.* 5 volumes. vol. 1: Burlington, Vt.: Miss A. M. Hemenway, 1867; vol. 2: Burlington, Vt.: Miss A. M. Hemenway, 1871; vol. 3: Claremont, N.H.: The Claremont Manufacturing Company, 1877; vol. 4: Montpelier, Vt.: Vermont Watchman and State Journal Press, 1882; vol. 5: Brandon, Vt.: Mrs. Carrie E. H. Page, 1891.

Historical Statistics of the United States, Colonial Times to 1970. 2 vols. Washington, D.C.: Bureau of the Census, Bicentennial edition, 1975.

Hodges, Graham R. *Root & Branch: African Americans in New York and East Jersey, 1613-1863.* Chapel Hill: University of North Carolina Press, 1999.

———. *Slavery and Freedom in the Rural North: African Americans in Monmouth County, New Jersey, 1665-1865*. Madison, Wisc.: Madison House, 1997.

Horton, James Oliver and Lois E. Horton. *In Hope of Liberty: Culture, Community and Protest Among Northern Free Blacks, 1700-1860*. New York: Oxford University Press, 1997.

Hubbard, Charles H. and Justus Dartt. *History of the Town of Springfield, Vermont*. Boston: George H. Walker & Co., 1895.

Jennings, Isaac. *Memorials of a Century*. Boston: Gould and Lincoln, 1869.

Jordan, Winthrop. *White Over Black: American Attitudes Toward the Negro, 1550-1812*. Chapel Hill: University of North Carolina Press, 1968.

Kaminski, John P. ed. *A Necessary Evil? Slavery and the Debate Over the Constitution*. Madison, Wisc.: Madison House, 1995.

Kolchin, Peter. *American Slavery, 1619-1877*. 1993; second edition, New York: Hill & Wang, 2003.

Lepore, Jill. *New York Burning: Liberty, Slavery, and Conspiracy in Eighteenth-Century Manhattan*. New York: Knopf, 2005.

Lin, Rachel C. "The Rhode Island Slave-Traders: Butchers, Bakers, and Candlestick-Makers." *Slavery and Abolition* 23 (December 2002): 21-38.

Litwack, Leon F. *North of Slavery: The Negro in the Free States, 1790-1860*. Chicago: University of Chicago Press, 1961.

Mackey, Frank. *Done With Slavery: The Black Fact in Montreal, 1760-1840*. Montreal and Kingston: McGill-Queen's University Press, 2010.

Manegold, C.S. *Ten Hills Farm: The Forgotten History of Slavery in the North*. Princeton, N.J.: Princeton University Press, 2010.

McConville, Brendan. "Of Slavery and Sources." *Reviews in American History* 34 (2006): 281-90.

McManus, Edgar J. *Black Bondage in the North*. Syracuse, N.Y.: Syracuse University Press, 1973.

Mello, Robert. *Moses Robinson and the Founding of Vermont*. Barre: Vermont Historical Society, forthcoming.

Menschel, David. "Abolition without Deliverance: The Law of Connecticut Slavery, 1784-1848." *Yale Law Review* 111 (2001): 183-222.

Middleton, Stephen, ed. *The Black Laws in the Old Northwest: A Documentary History*. Westport, Ct: Greenwood Press, 1993.

Morgan, Jennifer. *Laboring Women: Reproduction and Gender in New World Slavery*. Philadelphia: University of Pennsylvania Press, 2004.

Moss, Richard S. *Slavery on Long Island: A Study in Local Institutional and Early African American Communal Life*. New York: Garland, 1993.

Nash, Gary B. and Jean R. Soderlund, *Freedom by Degrees: Emancipation in Pennsylvania and its Aftermath*. New York: Oxford University Press, 1991.

Newell, Margaret E. "Indian Slavery in Colonial New England," in *Indian Slavery in Colonial America*, Alan Gallay, ed. Lincoln: University of Nebraska Press, 2009.

Onuf, Peter S. "State-Making in Revolutionary America: Independent Vermont as a Case Study." *Journal of American History* 67 (March 1981): 797-815.

Patterson, Orlando. *Slavery and Social Death: A Comparative Study*. Cambridge, Mass.: Harvard University Press, 1982.

Polgar, Paul. "'To Raise Them to an Equal Participation: Early National Abolitionism, Gradual Emancipation, and the Promise of African American Citizenship.'" *Journal of the Early Republic* 31 (Summer 2011): 229-58.

Risjord, Norman K. *Jefferson's America, 1760-1815*. Lanham, Md.: Rowman & Littlefield, 2010.

Roth, Eric J. "'The Society of Negroes Unsettled': A History of Slavery in New Paltz, N.Y." *Afro-Americans in New York Life and History* 27 (2003): 27-54.

Roth, Randolph A. *The Democratic Dilemma: Religion, Reform, and Social Order in the Connecticut River Valley of Vermont, 1791-1850*. Cambridge: Cambridge University Press, 1987.

Rothman, Adam. *Slave Country: American Expansion and the Origins of the Deep South*. Cambridge, Mass.: Harvard University Press, 2005.

Saillant, John. *Black Puritan, Black Republican: The Life and Thought of Lemuel Haynes, 1753-1833*. Oxford: Oxford University Press, 2003.

Soifer, Aviam. "De Facto Slavery and the 'Syren Songs of Liberty and Equality': Carol Weisbrod, Much Obliged." *Connecticut Law Review* 40(July 2008): 1317-1328.

Sherman, Michael, Gene Sessions, and P. Jeffrey Potash. *Freedom and Unity: A History of Vermont*. Barre: Vermont Historical Society, 2004.

Staudenraus, P. J. *The African Colonization Movement, 1816-1865*. New York: Columbia University Press, 1961.

Sweet, John W. *Bodies Politics: Negotiating Race in the American North, 1730-1830*. Baltimore: Johns Hopkins University Press, 2003.

Trudel, Marcel. *Dictionnaire des esclaves et de leurs proprietaries au Canada français*. Ville LaSalle: Hurtubise Cahiers du Québec, 1990.

True, Marshall M. "Slavery in Burlington? An Historical Note." *Vermont History* 50 (Fall 1982): 227-230.

Van Cleve, George W. *A Slaveholders' Union: Slavery, Politics, and the Constitution in the Early American Republic.* Chicago: University of Chicago Press, 2010.

Waldstreicher, David. *Slavery's Constitution: From Revolution to Ratification.* New York: Hill & Wang, 2009.

Wardner, H. S. "Judge Jacob and his Dinah." *The Vermonter* (May-June, 1914): 80-88.

West, Emily. *Family or Freedom: Free People of Color in the Antebellum South.* Lexington: University Press of Kentucky, 2012.

White, Shane. "Slavery in the North." *Magazine of History* 17 (2003): 17-21.

———. *Somewhat More Independent: The End of Slavery in New York City, 1770-1810.* Athens: University of Georgia Press, 1991.

Whitfield, Harvey Amani. "The Struggle Over Slavery in the Maritime Colonies." *Acadiensis* 41 (Summer/Autumn, 2012): 17-44.

Williamson, Jane. "Rowland T. Robinson, Rokeby, and the Underground Railroad in Vermont." *Vermont History* 69 (Winter 2001): 19-31.

Winter, Kari J. "The Strange Career of Benjamin Franklin Prentiss, Antislavery Lawyer." *Vermont History* 79 (Summer/Fall 2011): 121-40.

———. "Bordering Freedom but Unable to Cross into the Promised Land: Africans in Early Vermont." *Historical Reflections* 32 (2006): 473-92.

———. *The Blind African Slave: Or the Memoirs of Boyrereau Brinch, Nicknamed Jeffrey Brace.* Madison: University of Wisconsin Press, 2005.

Wood, Gordon S. *Empire of Liberty: A History of the Early Republic, 1789-1815.* New York: Oxford University Press, 2009.

———. *The Radicalism of the American Revolution.* New York: Alfred A. Knopf, 1992.

Zirblis, Raymond P. "Slavery in Vermont." In *The Vermont Encyclopedia*, John J. Duffy, Samuel B. Hand, and Ralph H. Orton, eds.. Hanover, N.H.: University Press of New England, 2003.

———. *Friends of Freedom: The Vermont Underground Railroad Survey.* Montpelier, Vt.: Division for Historic Preservation, 1996.

Zilversmit, Arthur. *The First Emancipation: The Abolition of Slavery in the North.* Chicago: University of Chicago Press, 1967.

Dissertations, Theses, Unpublished Papers

Graffagnino, J. Kevin. "Revolution and Empire on the Northern Frontier: Ira Allen of Vermont, 1751-1814." Ph.D. Dissertation, University of Massachusetts, 1993.

Guyette, Elise A. "Black Lives and White Racism in Vermont, 1760-1870."
Master's Thesis, University of Vermont, 1992.

Hannon, Matthew E. "From Vermont to Liberia: An Examination of the
Vermont Colonization Society." Master's Thesis, University of Vermont,
2008.

MacCabe, Alistair W. W. "The Story of the No-Slavery Clause of the Repub-
lic of Vermont, 1777." Unpublished undergraduate paper, Eisenhower
College, 1971. Vermont State Archives and Records Administration,
Middlesex.

Polgar, Paul. "Standard Bearers of Liberty and Equality: Reinterpreting the
Origins of American Abolitionism." Ph.D. Dissertation, CUNY Graduate Center, 2013.

Stone, Carolyn. "A Monograph on an Act Introduced in the Vermont General Assembly on 24 January 1791 Respecting Negr[oes] & Molattoes."
Unpublished paper, Vermont State Archives and Records Administration, Middlesex.

Watson, John H. "In Re Vermont Constitution of 1777, as Regards its Adoption, and its Declaration Forbidding Slavery; and the Subsequent Existence of Slavery Within the Territory of the Sovereign State," an address
delivered to the Vermont Bar Association, January 4, 1921.

Zirblis, Raymond P. "A Grain of Salt: Slavery in Vermont's Colonial and
Early Statehood Eras." Paper presented at the Center for Research on
Vermont, University of Vermont, Burlington, February 4, 2009.

Index

Harvey Amani Whitfield is an Associate Professor of History at the University of Vermont. His areas of research are the black populations of the Maritime colonies and Vermont. He is the author of *Blacks on the Border: The Black Refugees in British North America, 1815-1860* (University Press of New England, 2006).
He has also published numerous articles and book reviews, including "The Struggle Over Slavery in the Maritime Colonies," *Acadiensis: Journal of the History of the Atlantic Region*, 41 (Autumn 2012).